Radnor Forest from the northern slopes of Hawthorn Hill (Stage 5)

OFFA'S DYKE PATH

This guidebook describes Offa's Dyke Path National Trail, a 177-mile (285km) long-distance route along the English–Welsh border between Sedbury (near Chepstow) and Prestatyn on the North Wales coast. One of Britain's classic trails, this ancient route is long but not particularly strenuous, making it an ideal challenge for first-time backpackers.

Contents and using this guide

This booklet of Ordnance Survey 1:25,000 Explorer maps has been designed for convenient use on the trail and includes:
- a key to map pages (page 3) showing where to find the maps for each stage.
- the full and up-to-date line of the National Trail
- an extract from the OS Explorer map legend (pages 76–78).

In addition, the companion *Offa's Dyke Path* guidebook describes the full route from south to north, alongside all the information you need to plan a successful trip and lots of incidental information about local history, geography and wildlife.

© Cicerone Press 2016
Reprinted 2019, 2021, 2023
ISBN-13: 978 1 85284 894 1
Photos © Chris & Mike Dunn 2016

@ Crown copyright and database rights 2016
OS PU100012932

OFFA'S DYKE PATH

Stage 1	Sedbury to Monmouth	4
Stage 2	Monmouth to Pandy	10
Stage 3	Pandy to Hay-on-Wye	15
Stage 4	Hay-on-Wye to Kington	24
Stage 5	Kington to Knighton	29
Stage 6	Knighton to Brompton Bridge	34
Stage 7	Brompton Bridge to Buttington	39
Stage 8	Buttington to Llanymynech	44
Stage 9	Llanymynech to Castle Mill	49
Stage 10	Castle Mill to Llandegla	54
Stage 11	Llandegla to Bodfari	61
Stage 12	Bodfari to Prestatyn	69

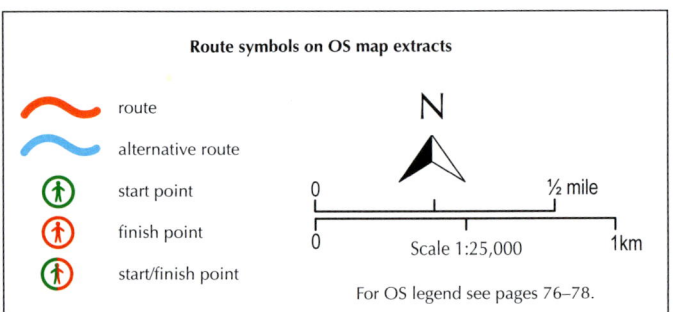

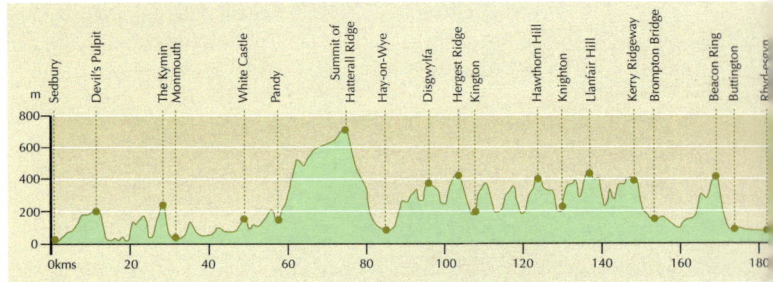

Offa's Dyke Path

IRISH SEA

— Offa's Dyke Path
↑ direction of route in this booklet

- Prestatyn 68–74
- Denbigh
- Ruthin 61–68
- Clwydian Range
- Wrexham
- 54–61
- Llangollen
- 49–54
- SNOWDONIA
- Oswestry
- 44–49
- WALES
- ENGLAND
- Shrewsbury
- Welshpool
- 39–44
- Montgomery
- Shropshire Hills
- Clun
- 34–39
- Ludlow
- Knighton
- 29–34
- Kington
- 24–29
- Hay-on-Wye
- Hereford
- Wye Valley
- 15–24
- 10–15
- BRECON BEACONS
- Abergavenny
- Monmouth
- Gloucester
- 4–9
- Newport
- Chepstow
- CARDIFF
- BRISTOL CHANNEL
- BRISTOL
- LIVERPOOL

Elevation profile labels: Moelydd, Selattyn Hill, Castle Mill, River Dee, Llandegla Forest / Llandegla, Moel Famau, Bodfari, Marian Ffrith, Prestatyn

200 220 240 260 280

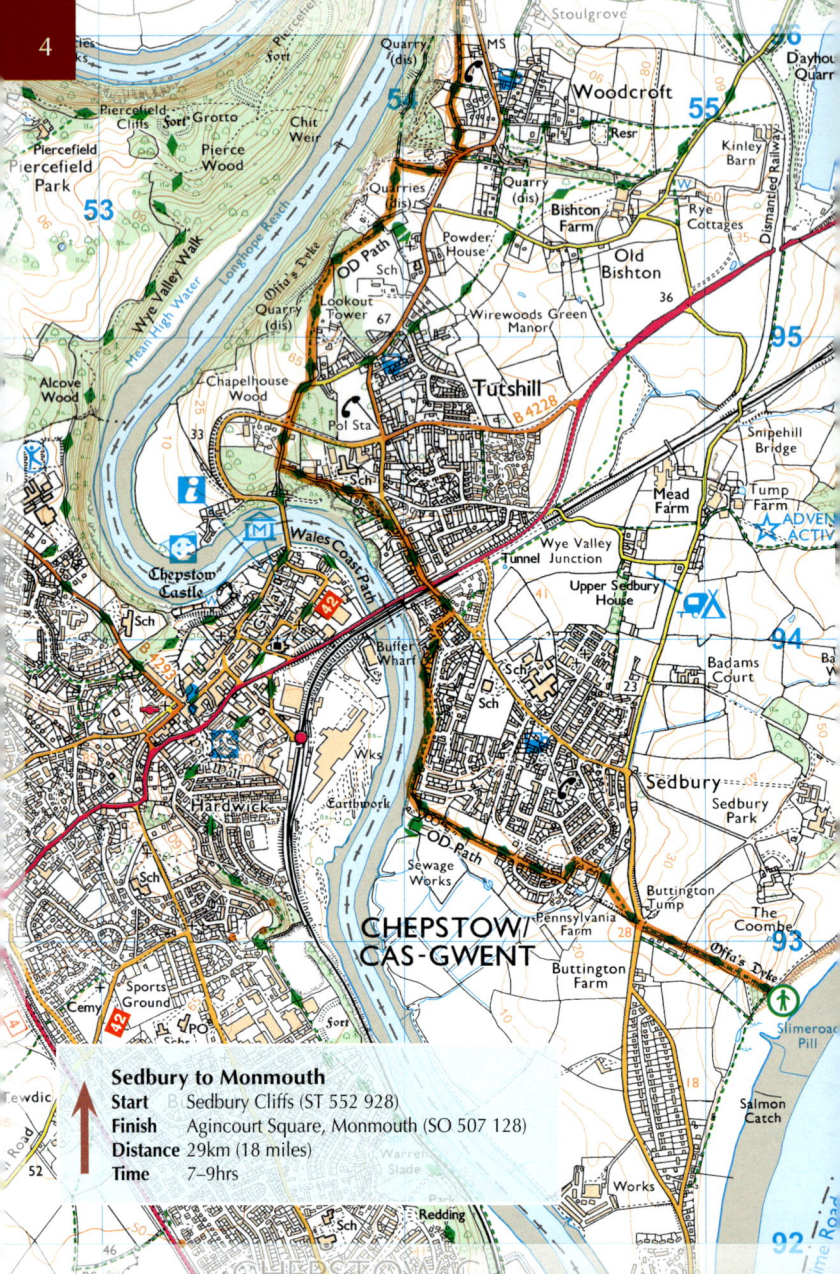

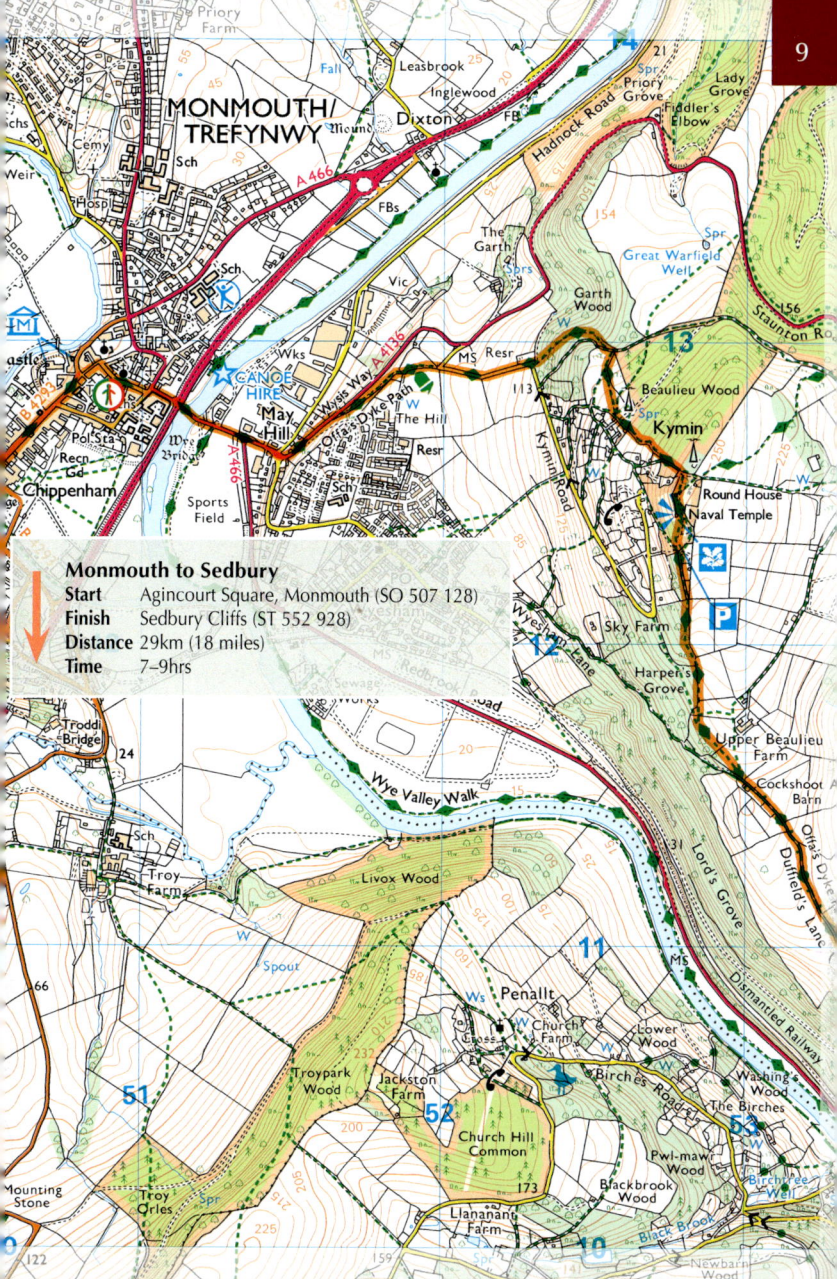

Monmouth to Sedbury
Start   Agincourt Square, Monmouth (SO 507 128)
Finish   Sedbury Cliffs (ST 552 928)
Distance 29km (18 miles)
Time   7–9hrs

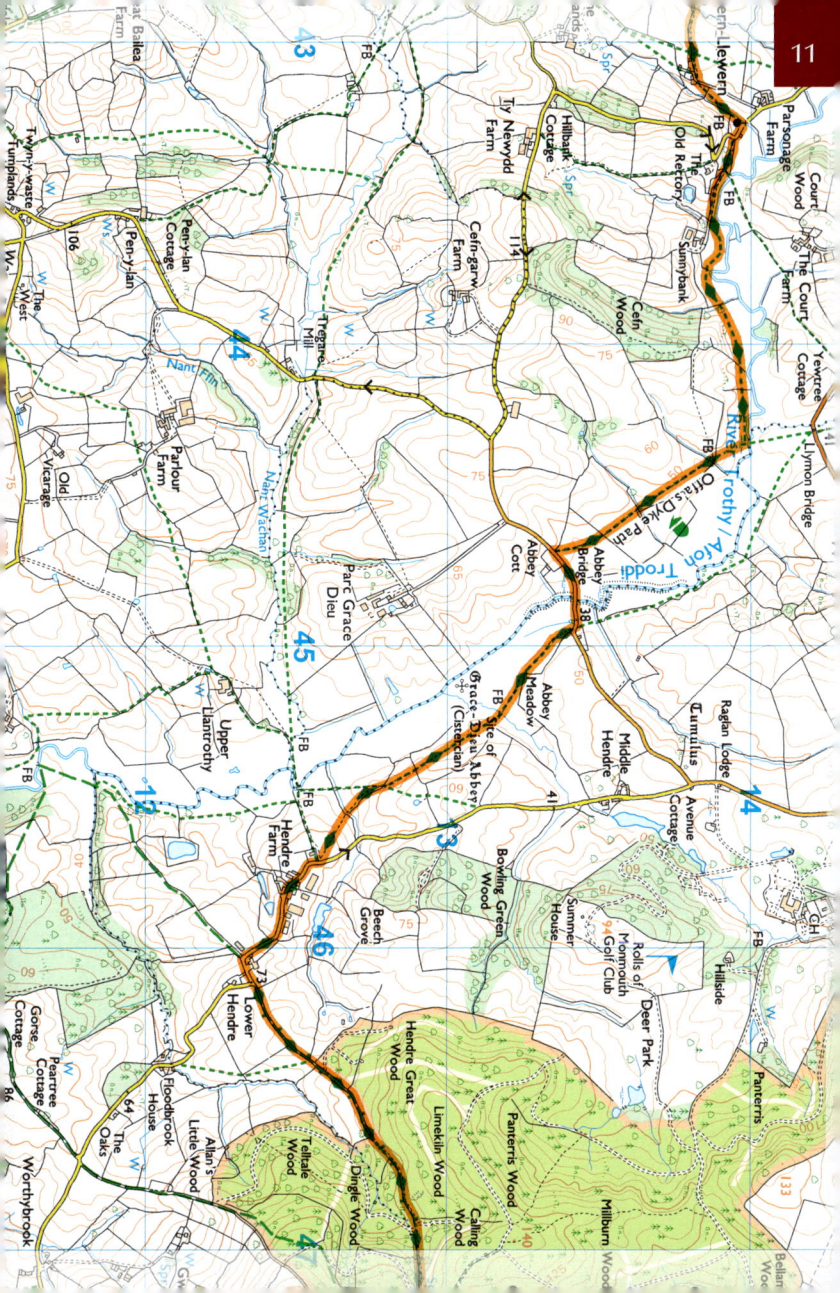

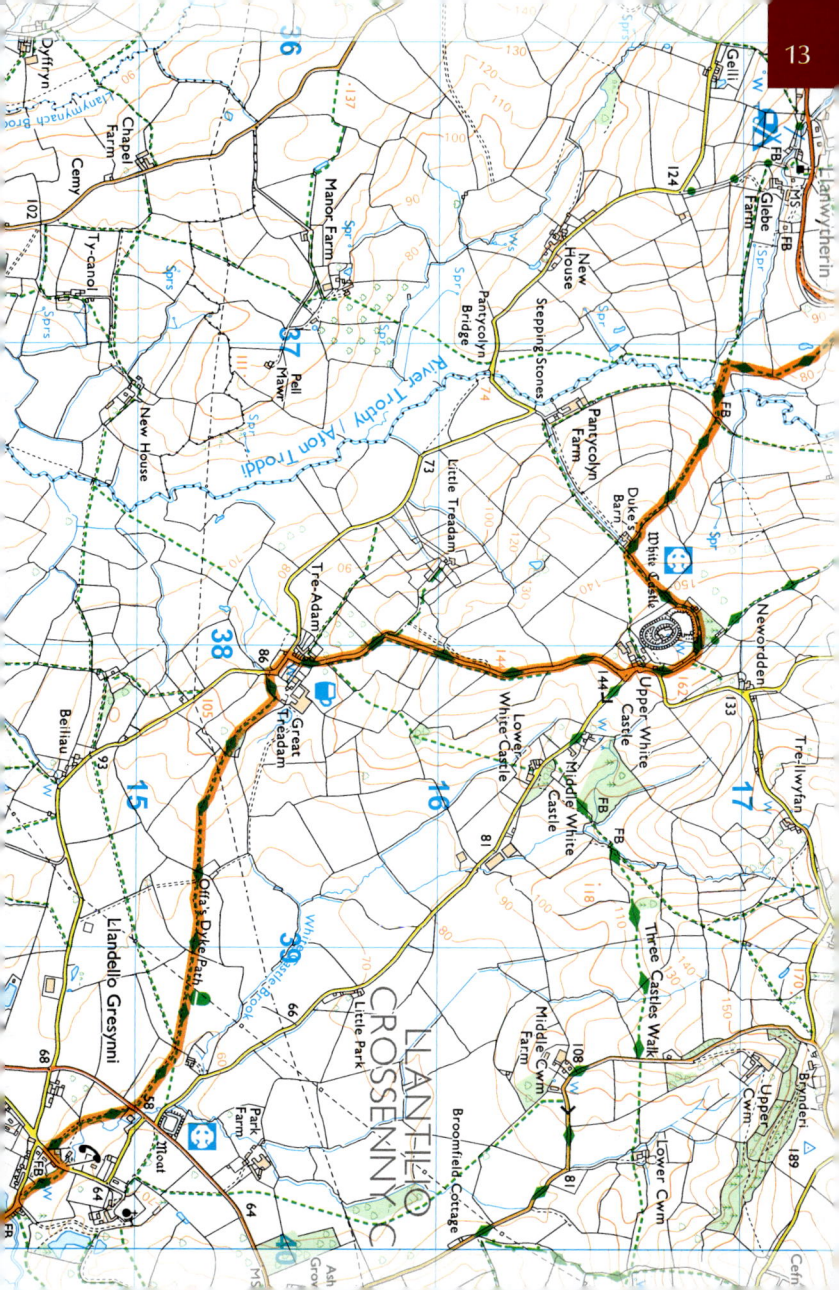

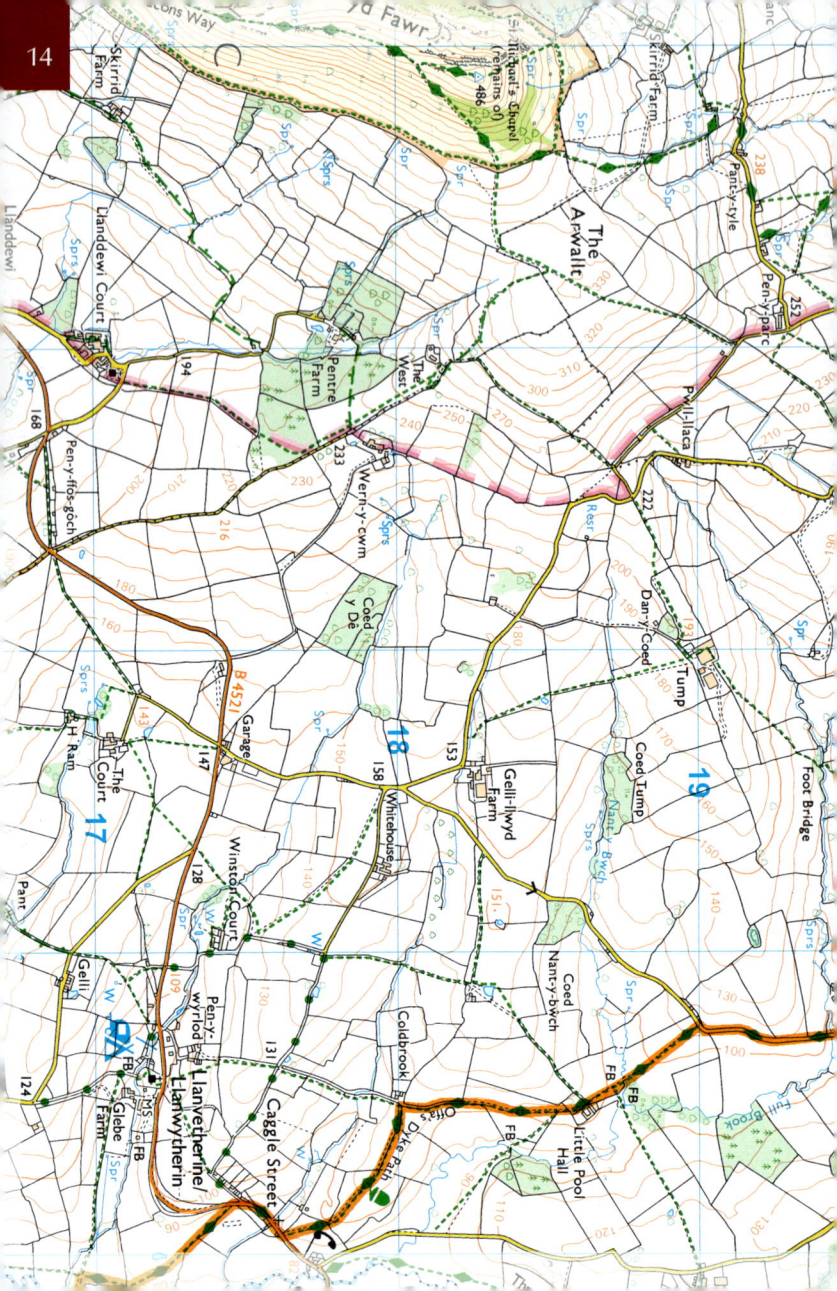

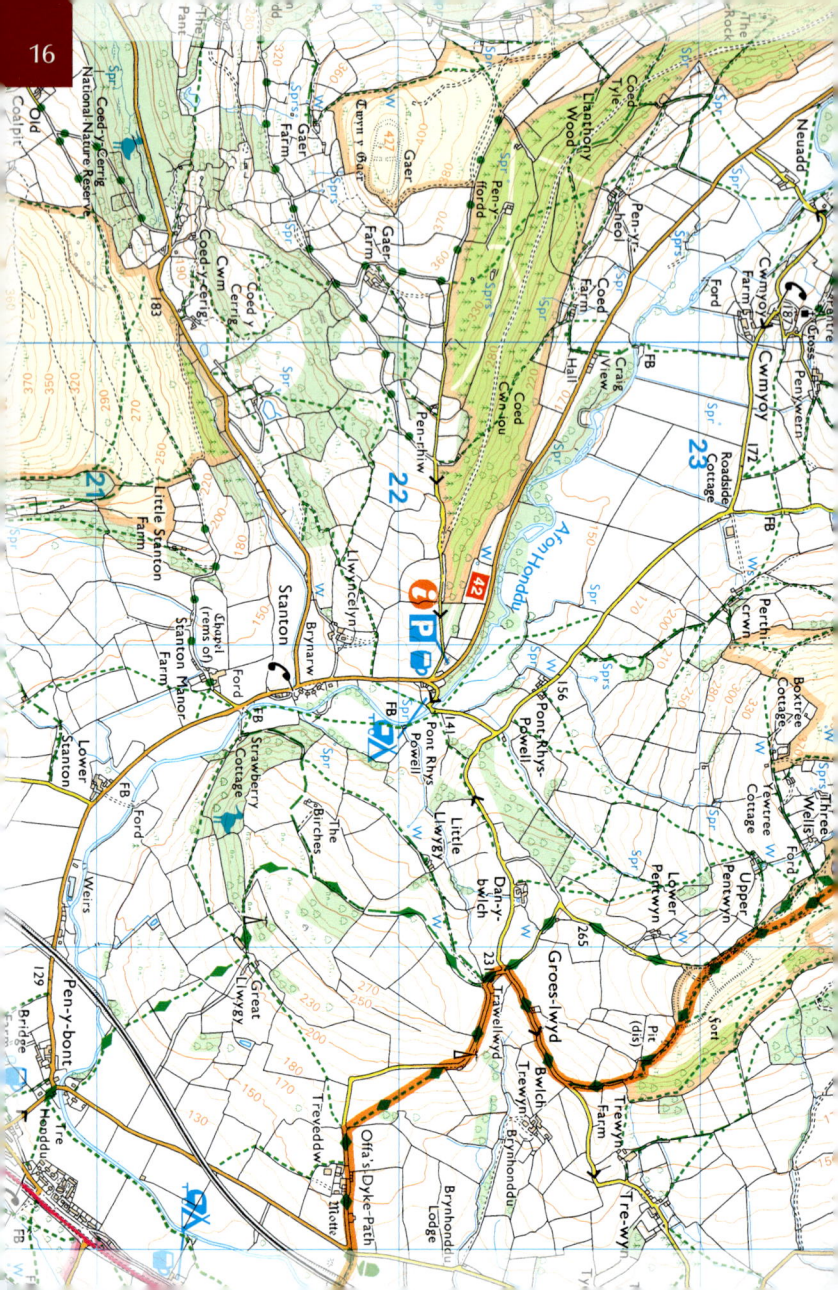

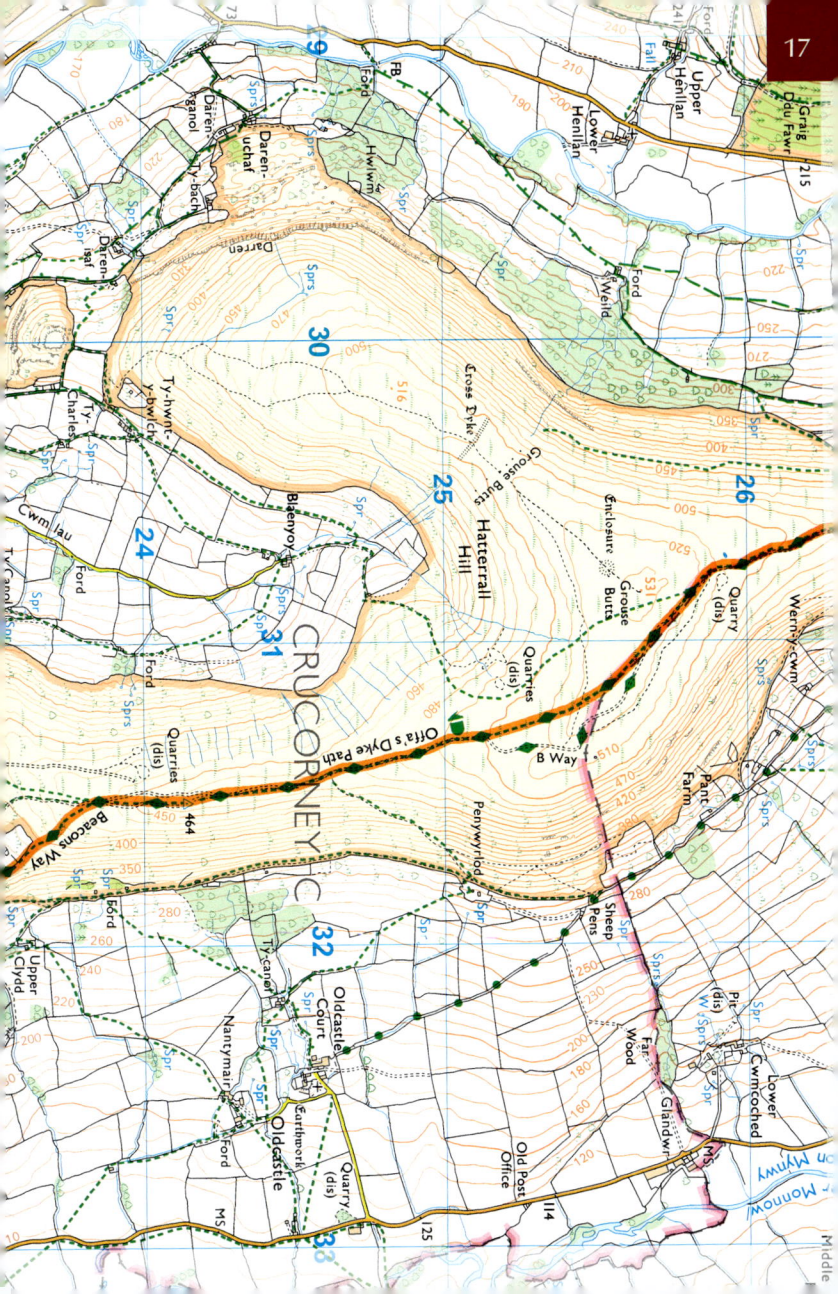

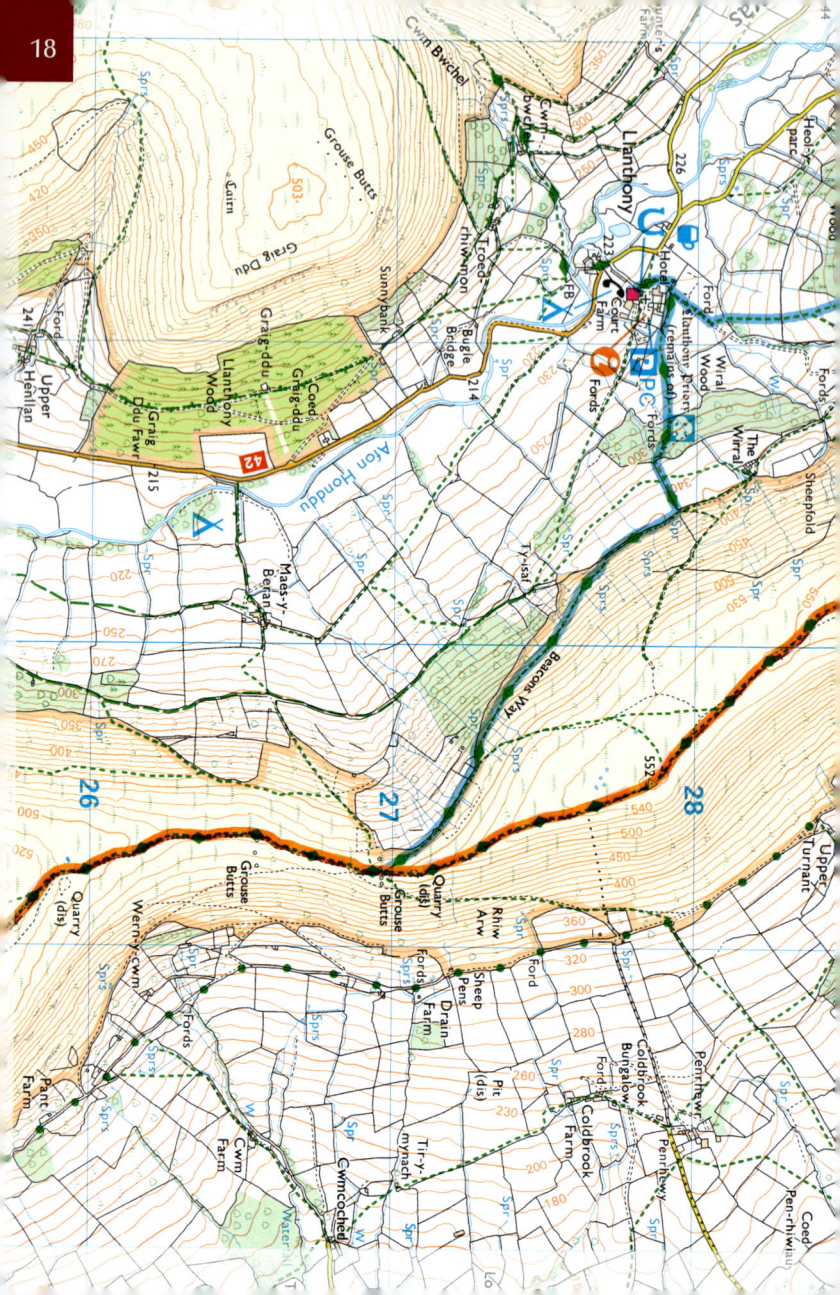

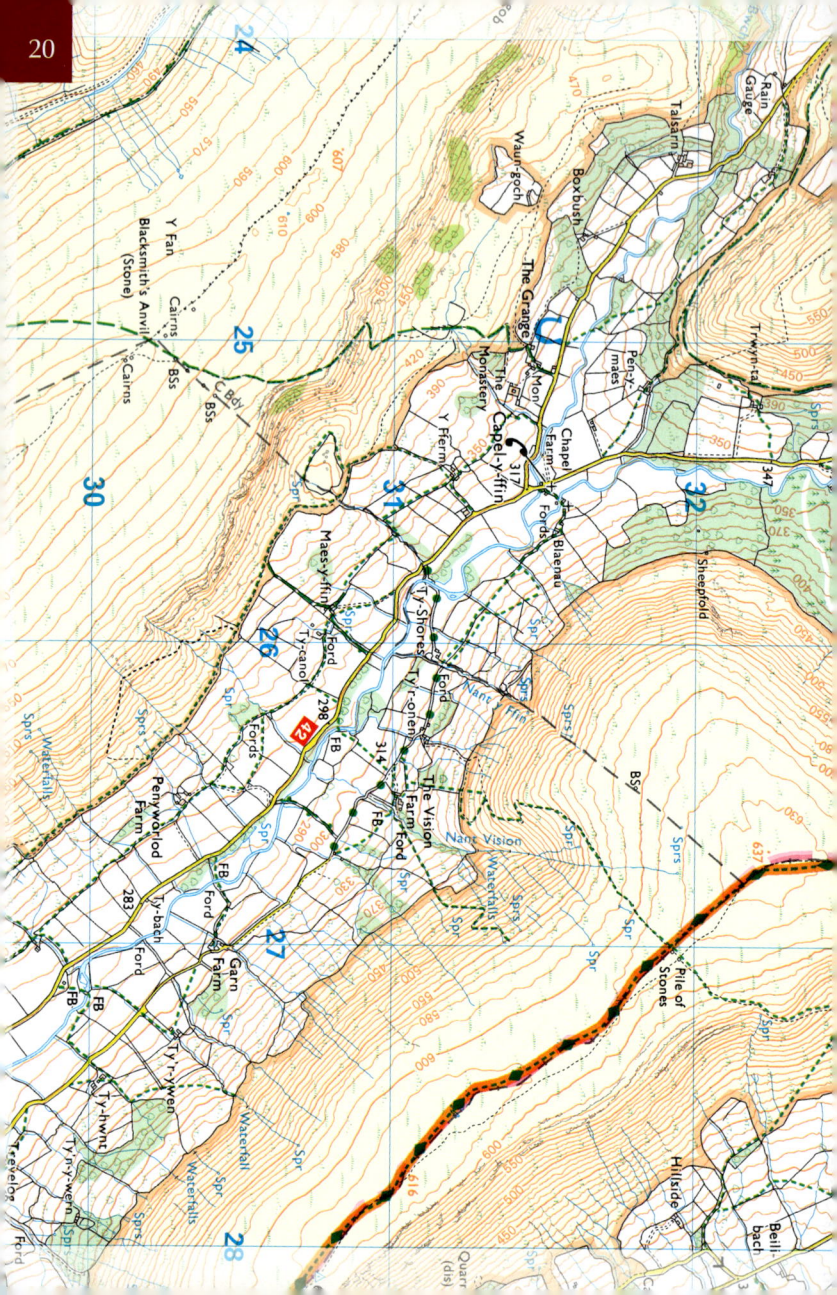

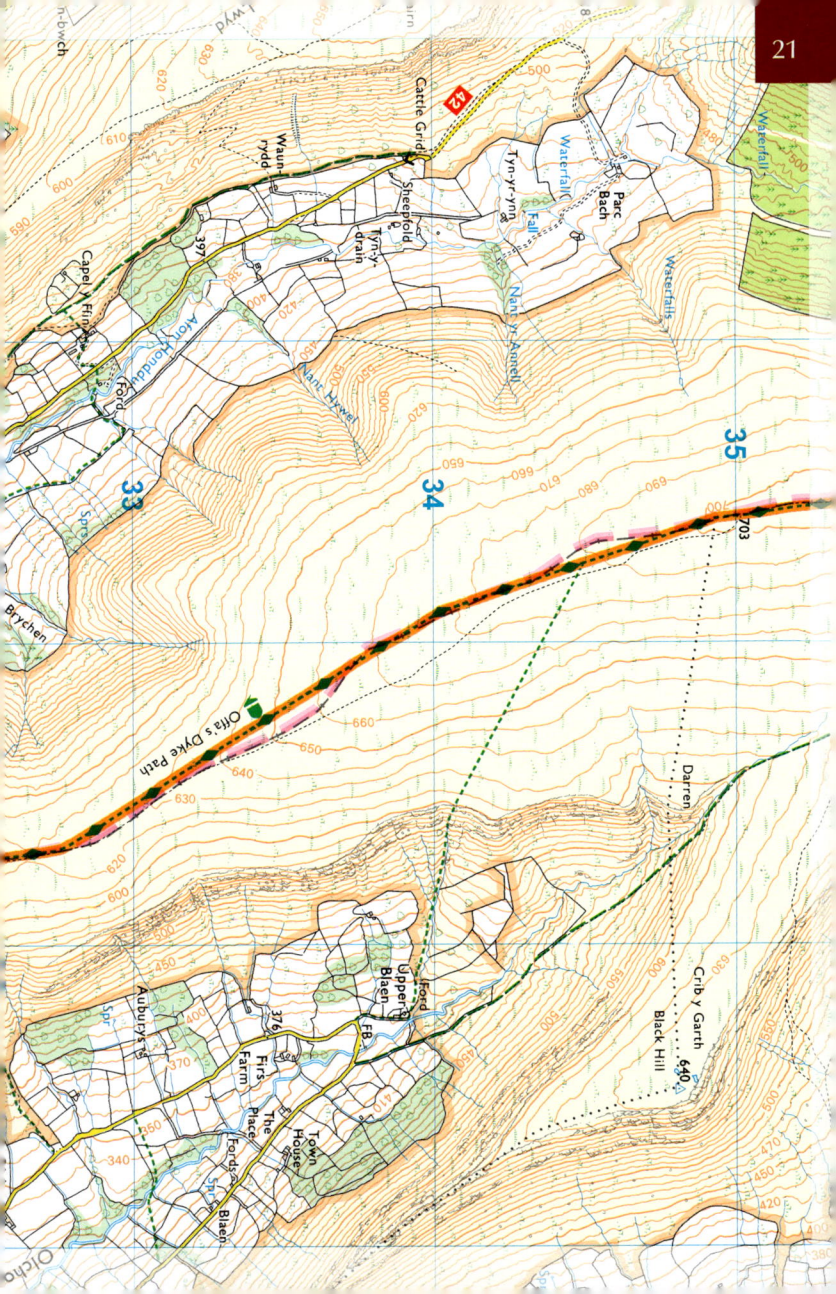

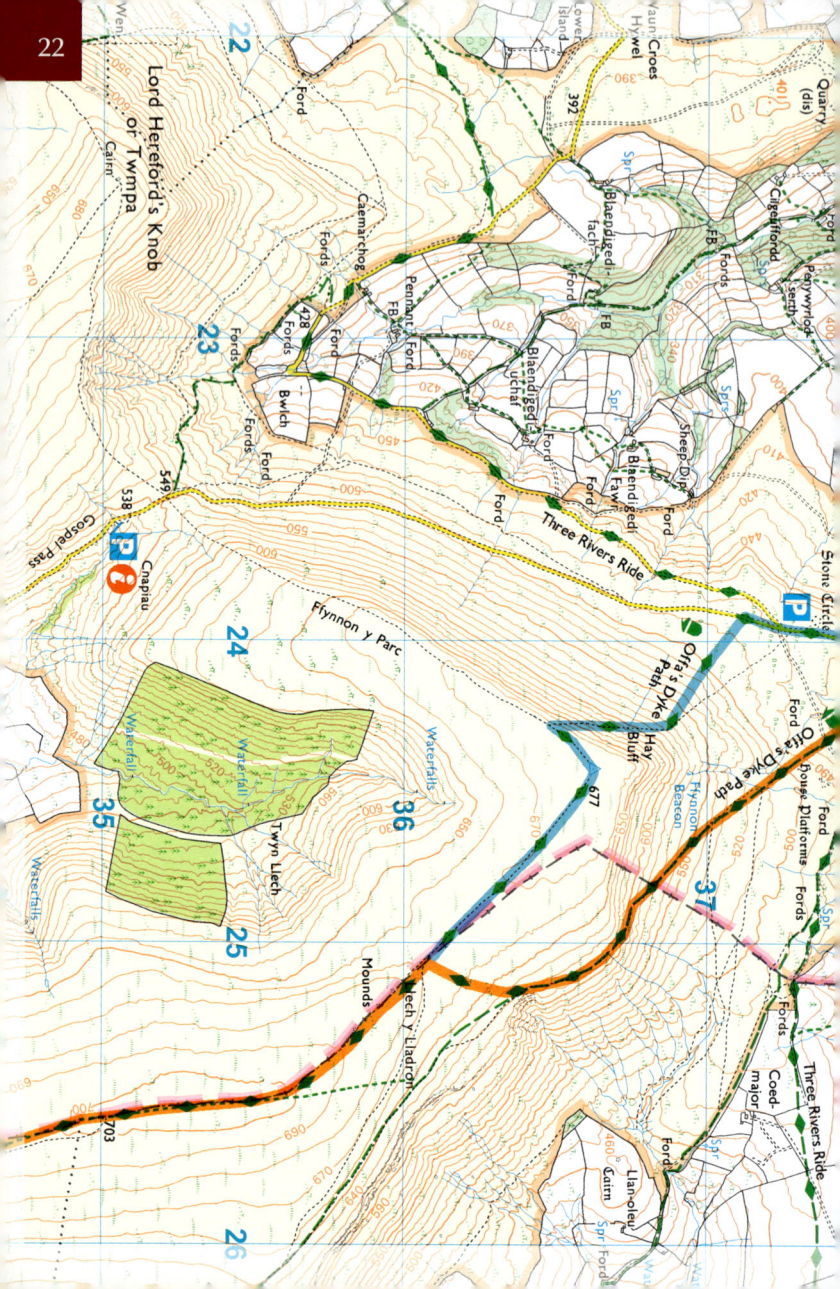

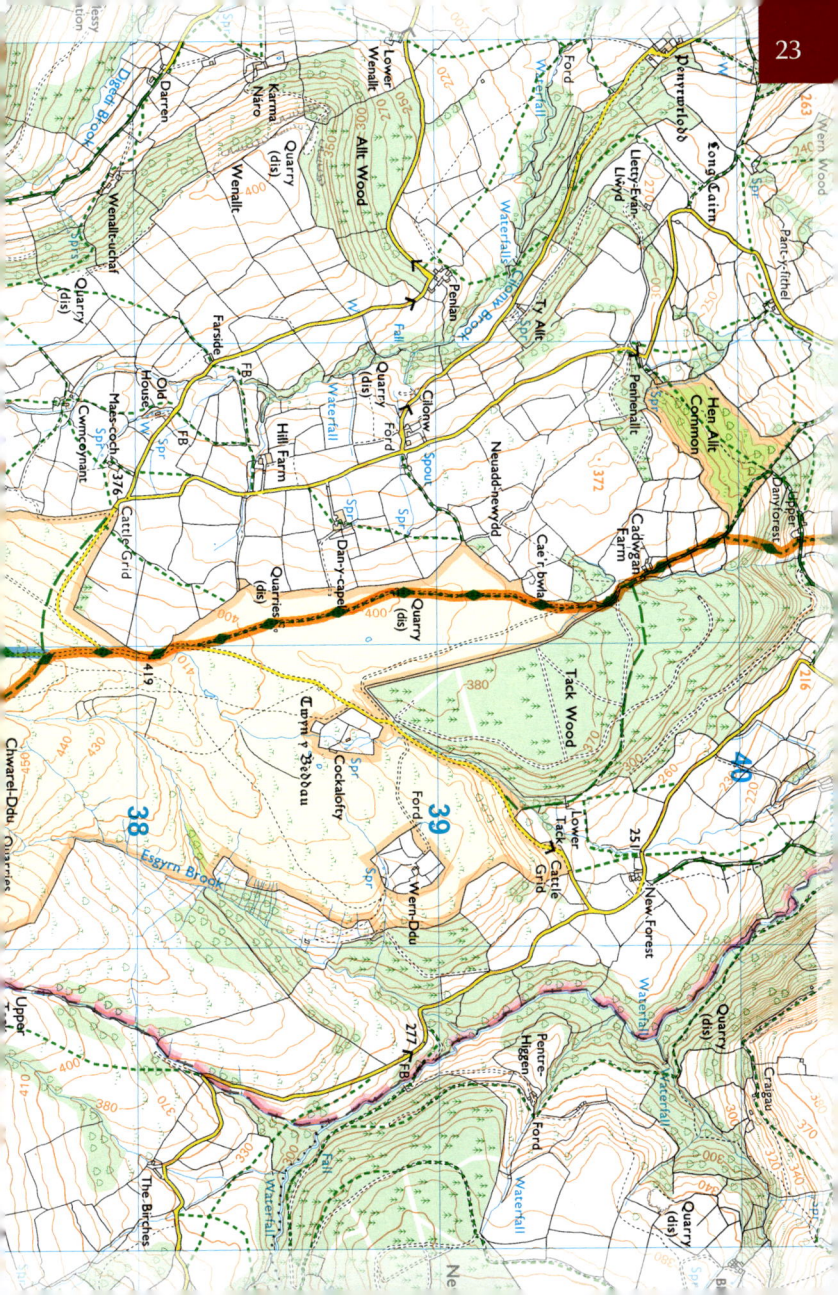

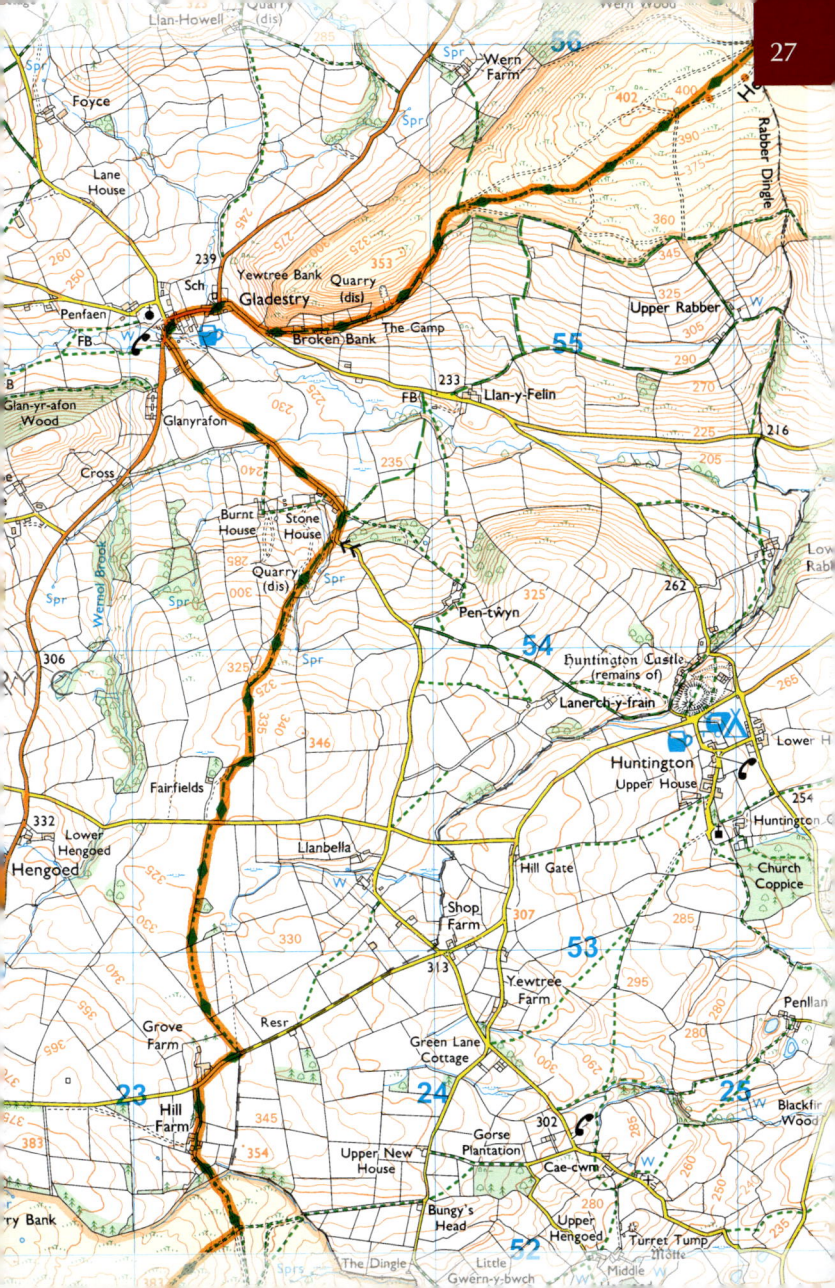

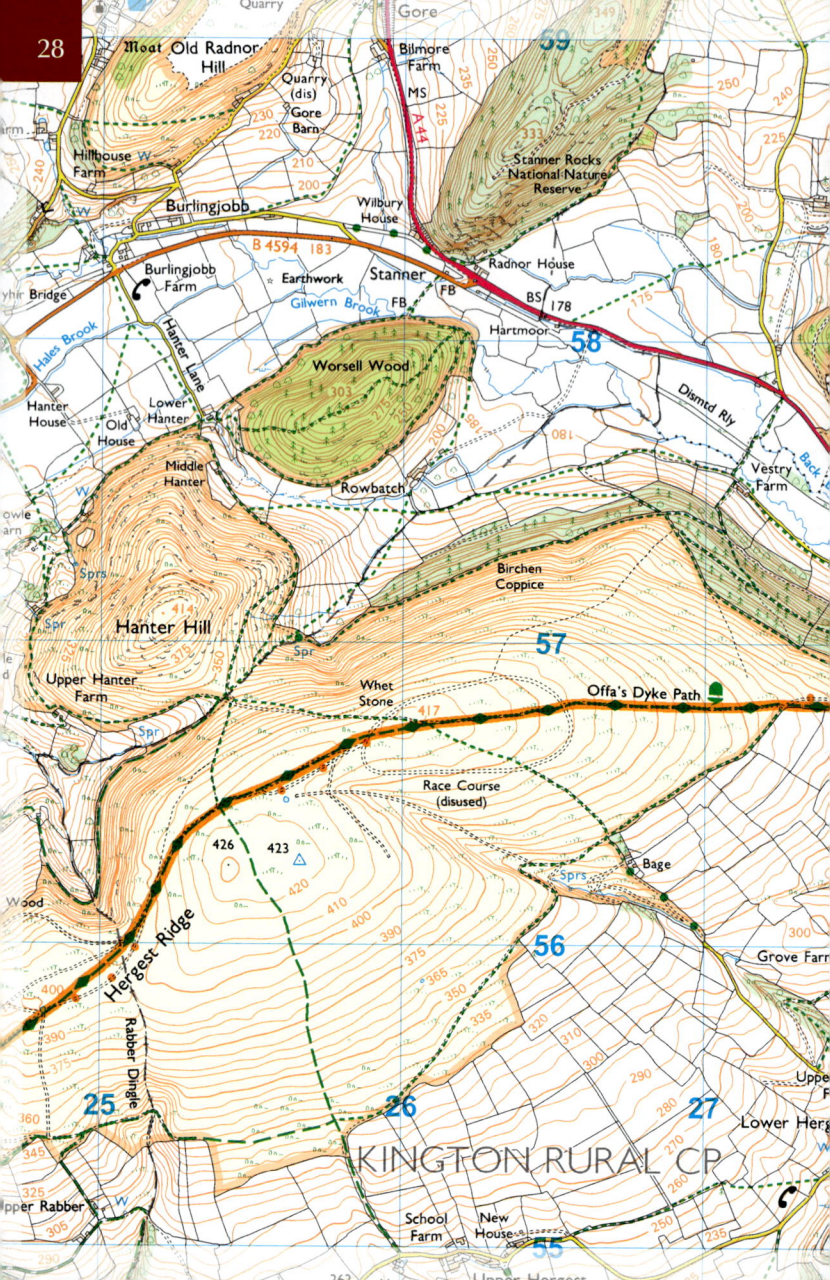

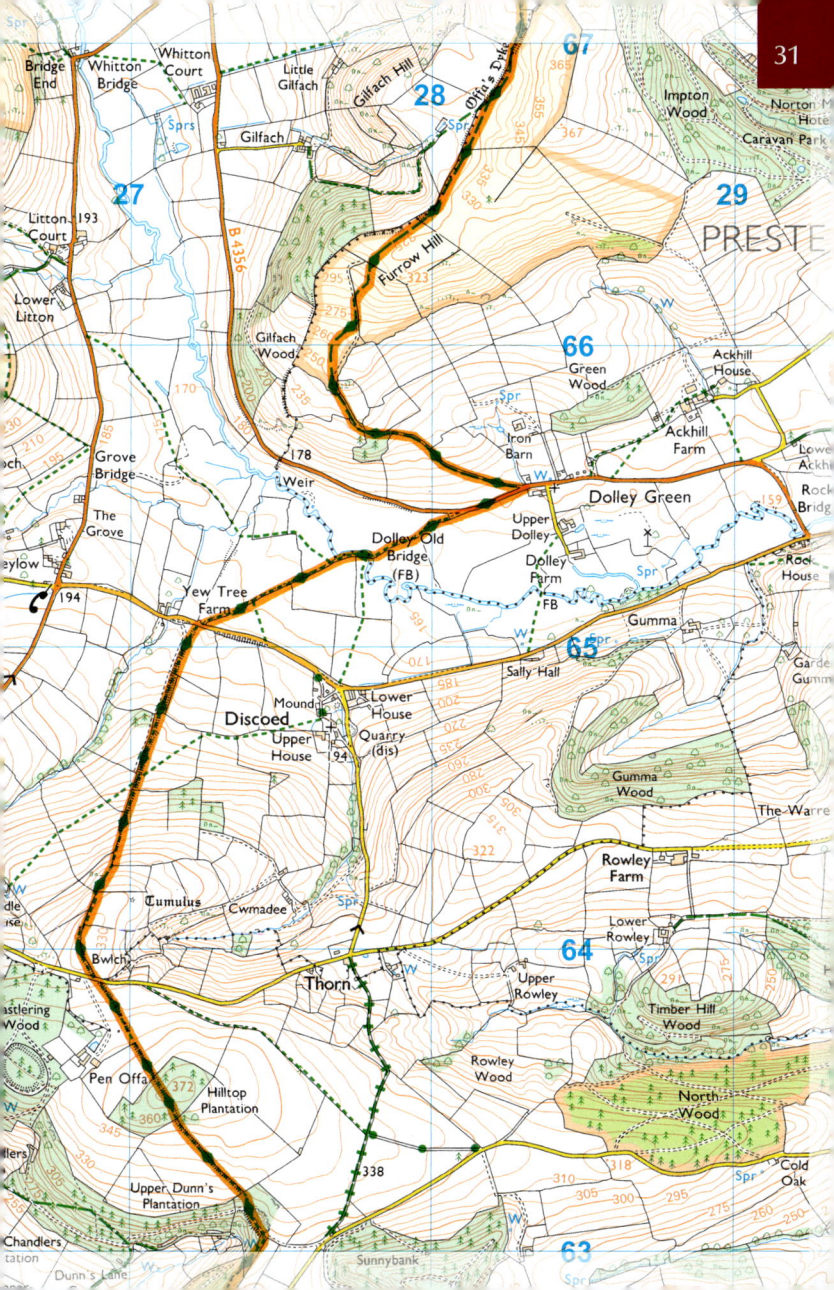

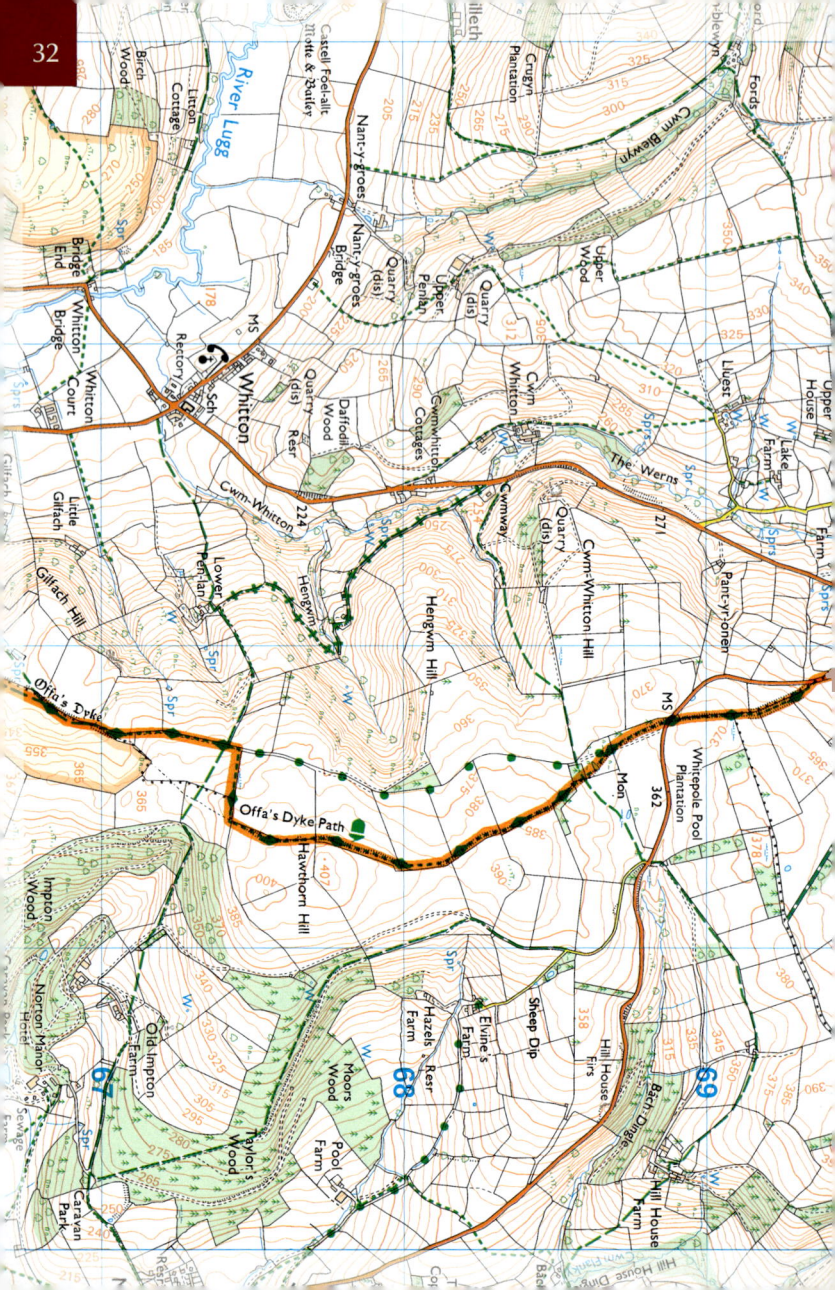

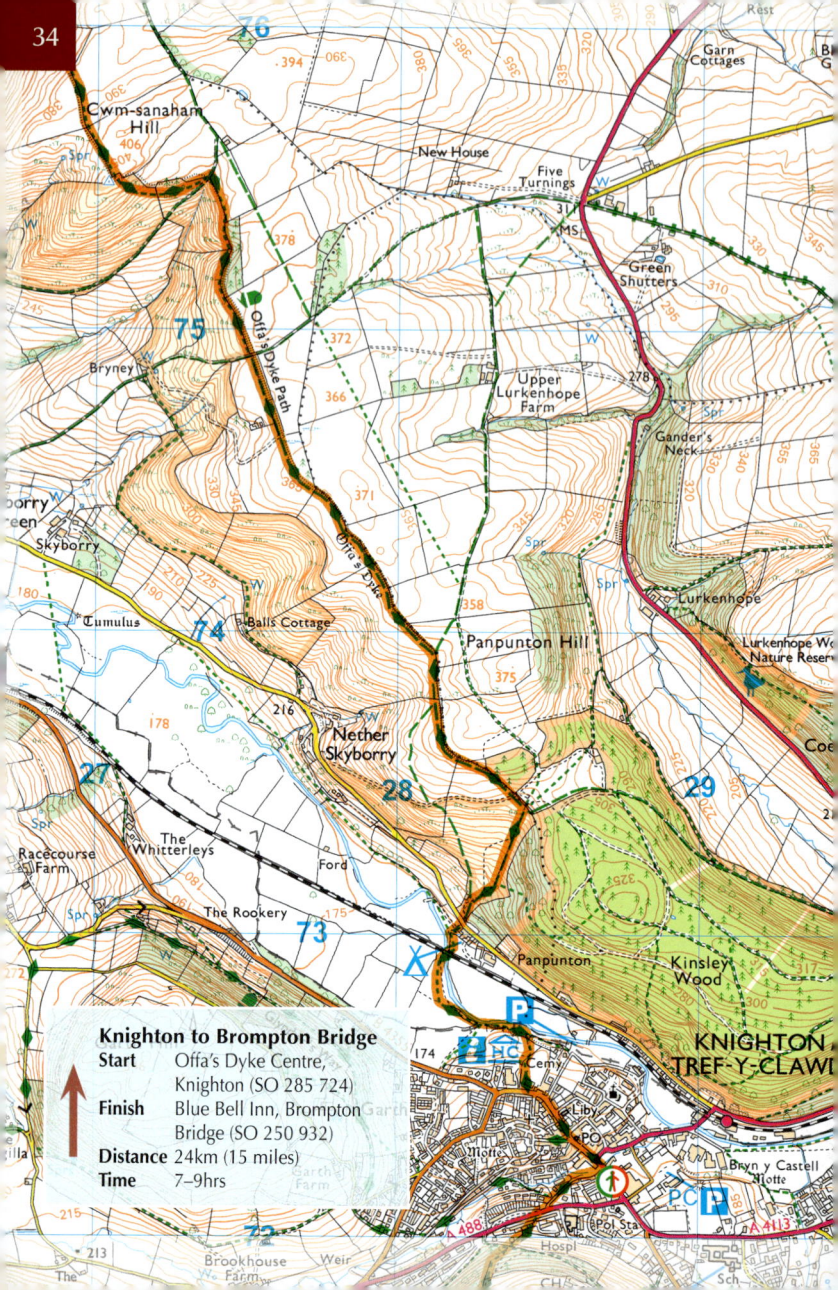

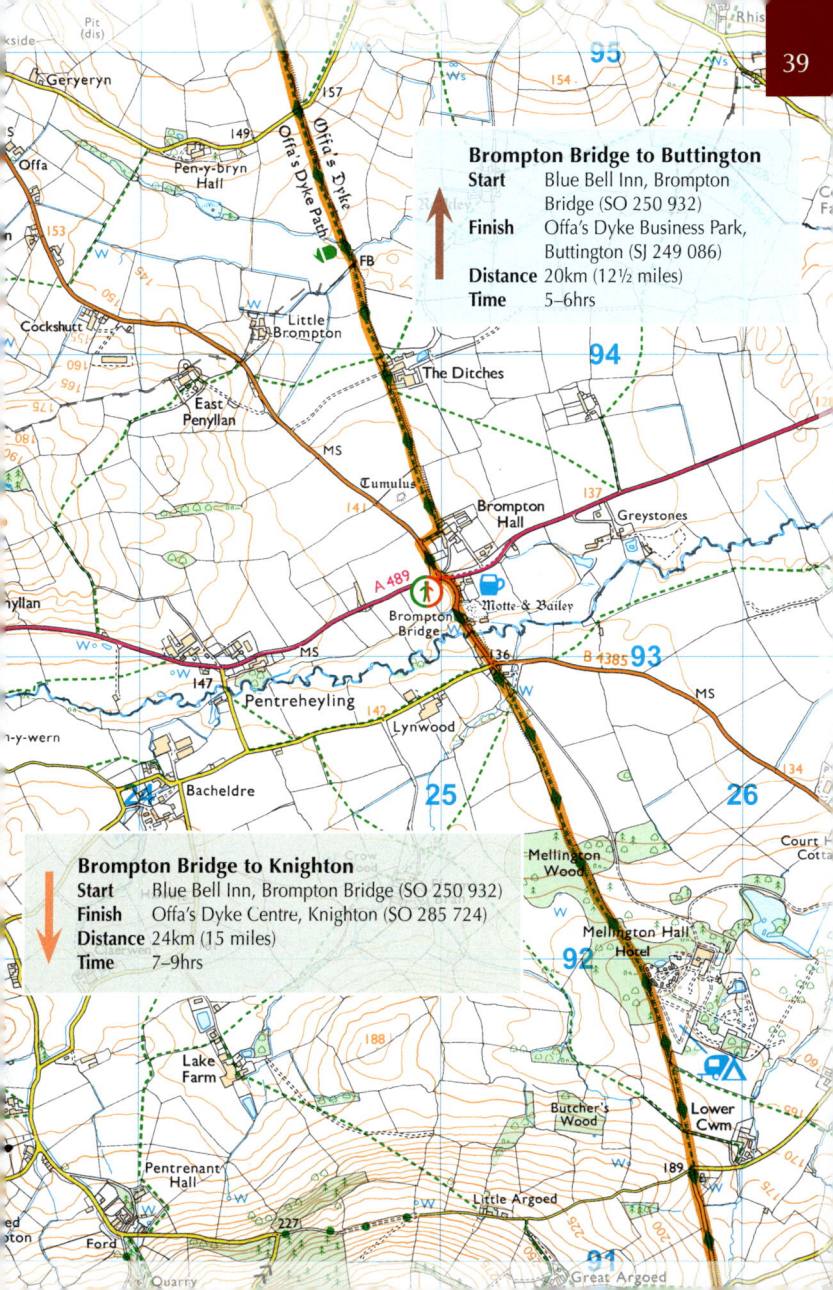

Brompton Bridge to Buttington
Start   Blue Bell Inn, Brompton Bridge (SO 250 932)
Finish   Offa's Dyke Business Park, Buttington (SJ 249 086)
Distance 20km (12½ miles)
Time   5–6hrs

Brompton Bridge to Knighton
Start   Blue Bell Inn, Brompton Bridge (SO 250 932)
Finish   Offa's Dyke Centre, Knighton (SO 285 724)
Distance 24km (15 miles)
Time   7–9hrs

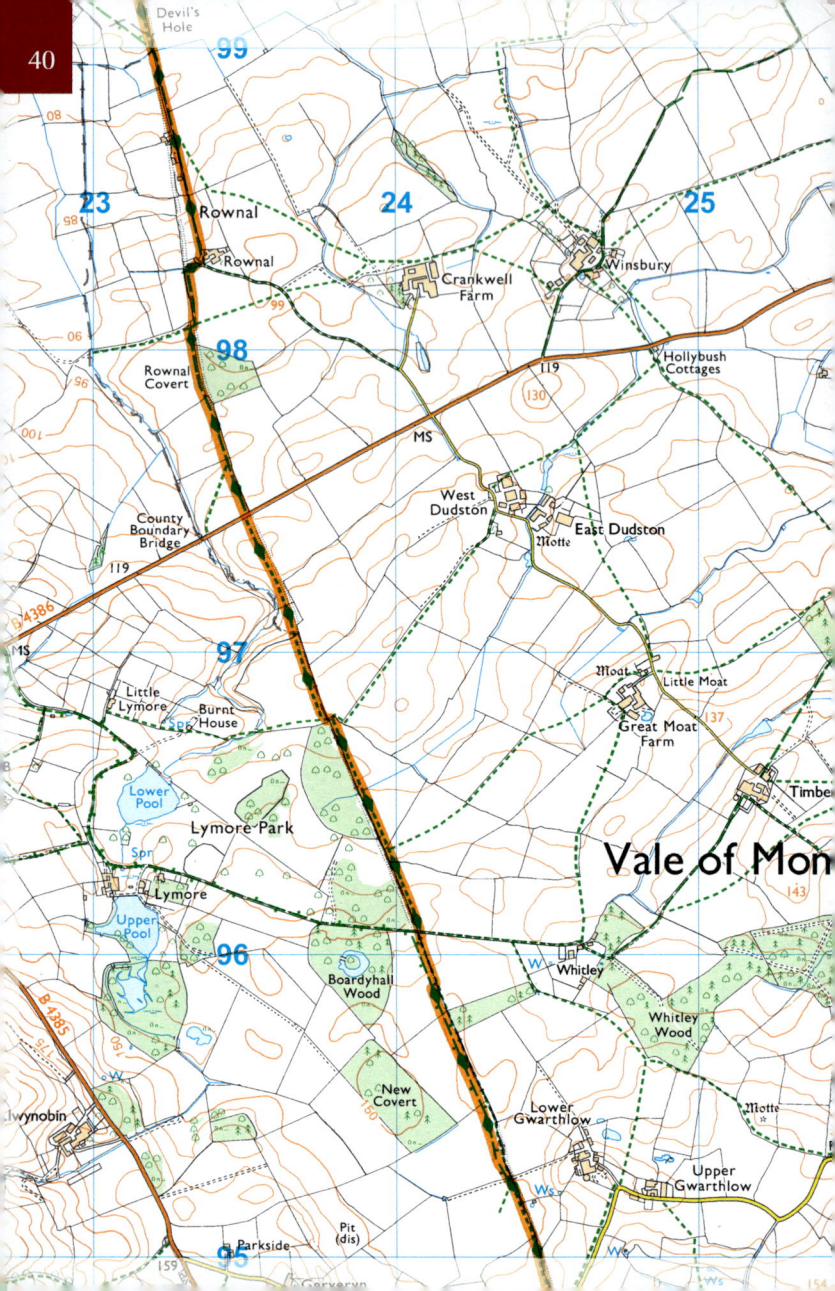

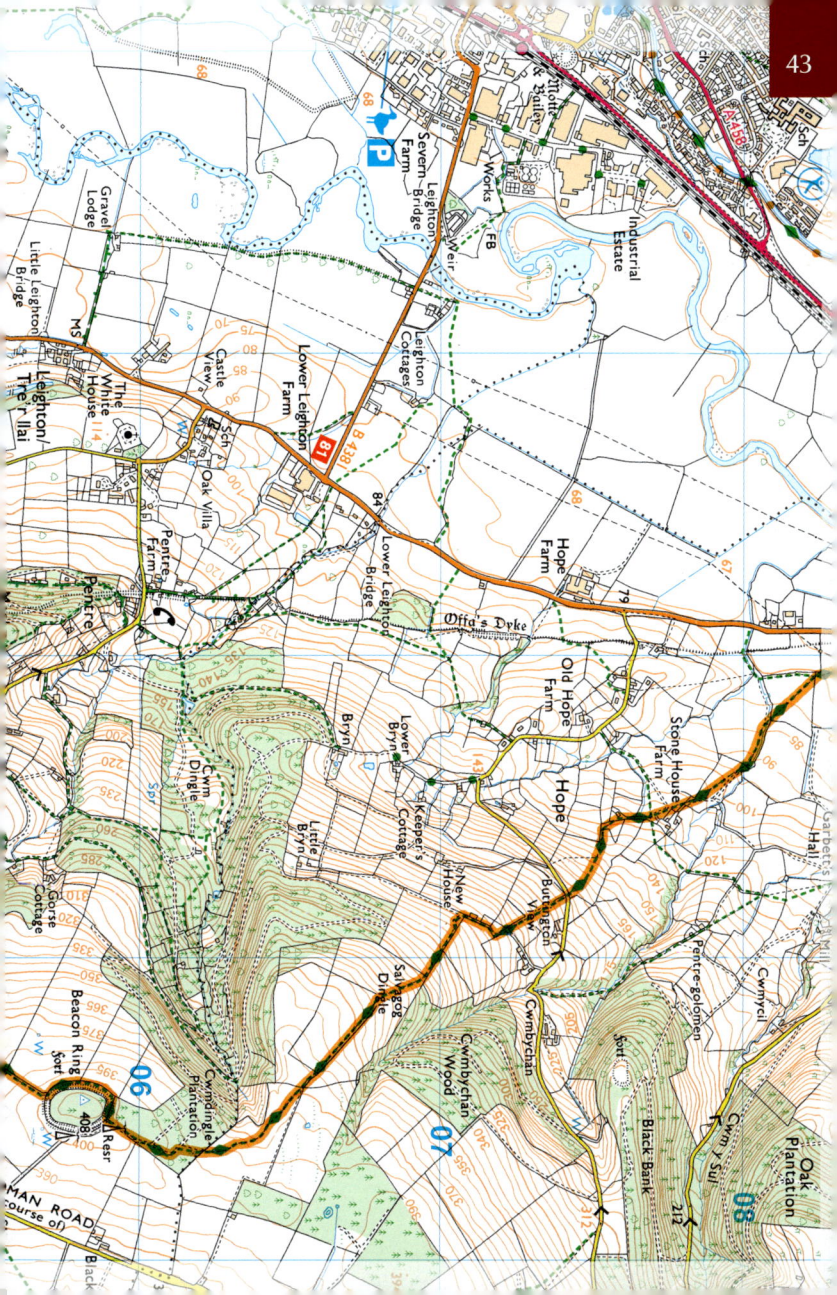

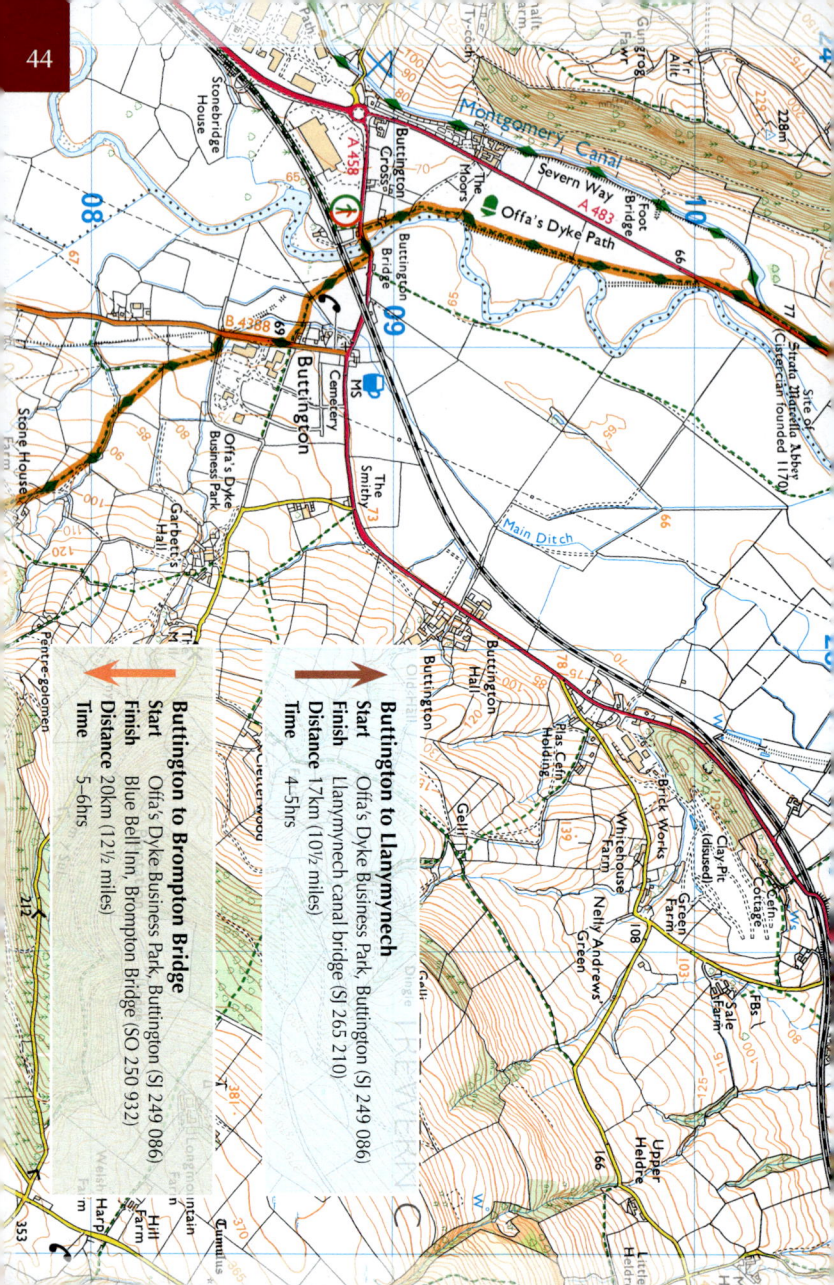

Buttington to Llanymynech

Start Offa's Dyke Business Park, Buttington (SJ 249 086)
Finish Llanymynech canal bridge (SJ 265 210)
Distance 17km (10½ miles)
Time 4–5hrs

Buttington to Brompton Bridge

Start Offa's Dyke Business Park, Buttington (SJ 249 086)
Finish Blue Bell Inn, Brompton Bridge (SO 250 932)
Distance 20km (12½ miles)
Time 5–6hrs

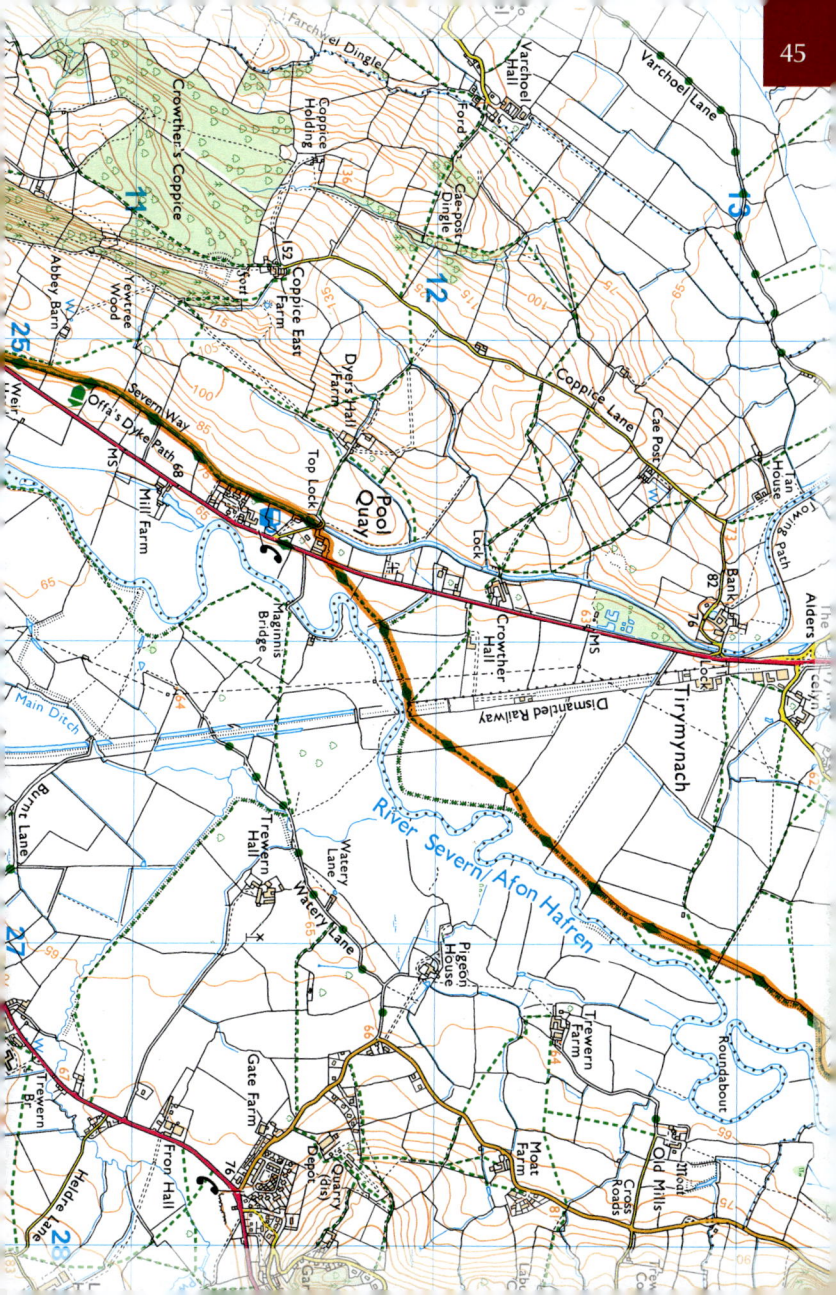

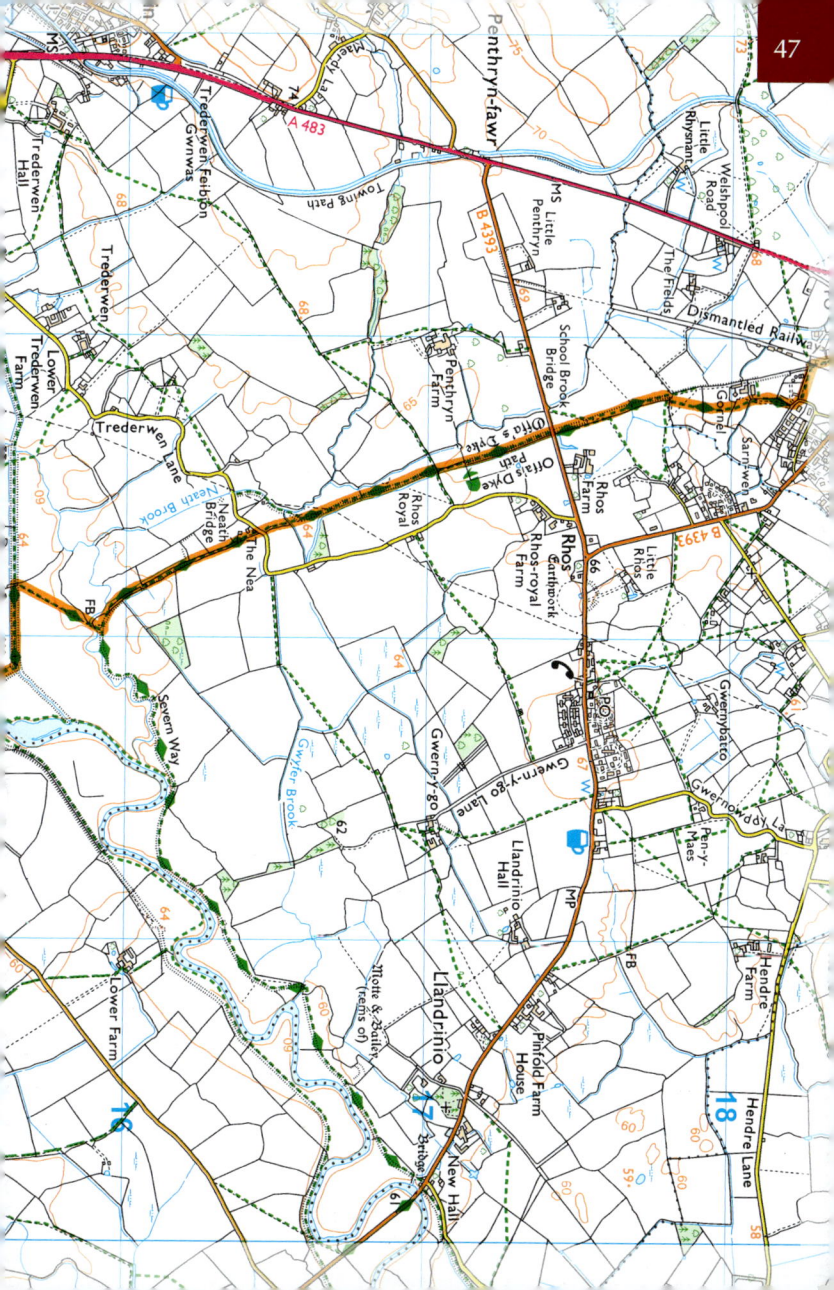

Llanymynech to Buttington
Start Llanymynech canal bridge (SJ 265 210)
Finish Offa's Dyke Business Park, Buttington (SJ 249 086)
Distance 17km (10½ miles)
Time 4–5hrs

Llanymynech to Castle Mill
Start Llanymynech canal bridge (SJ 265 210)
Finish Castle Mill, Chirk (SJ 262 377)
Distance 22km (13½ miles)
Time 6–7hrs

Castle Mill to Llanymynech
Start Castle Mill, Chirk (SJ 262 377)
Finish Llanymynech canal bridge (SJ 265 210)
Distance 22km (13½ miles)
Time 6–7hrs

Castle Mill to Llandegla
Start Castle Mill, Chirk (SJ 262 377)
Finish Llandegla church (SJ 195 524)
Distance 24km (15 miles)
Time 6–8hrs

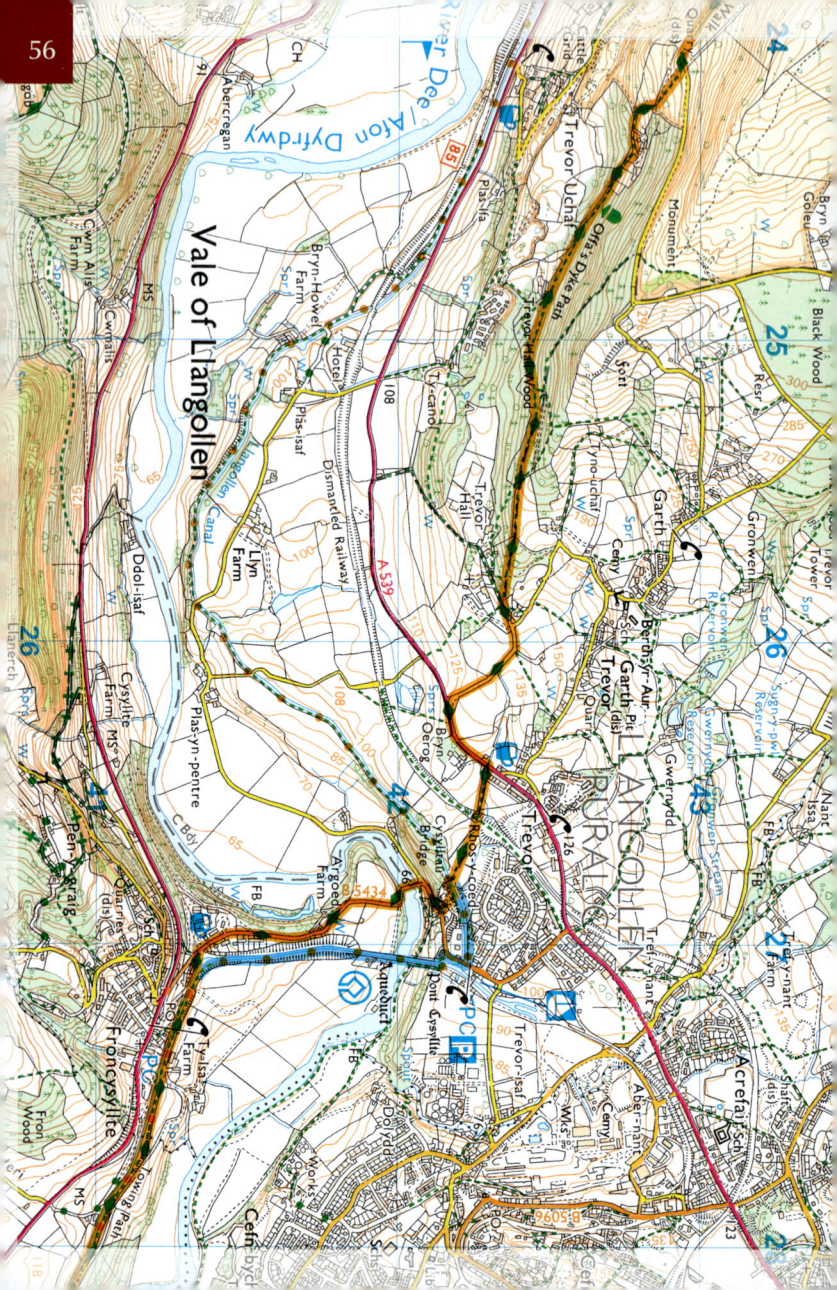

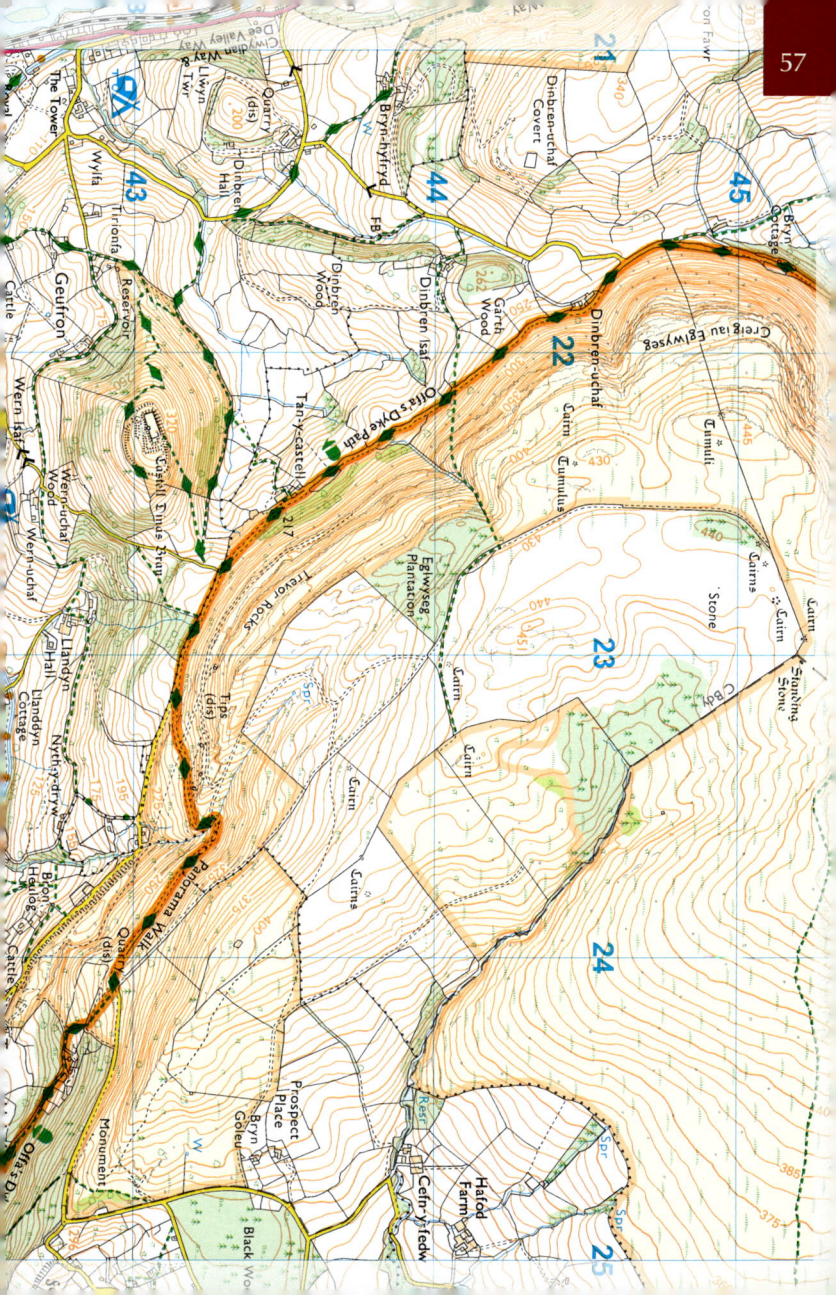

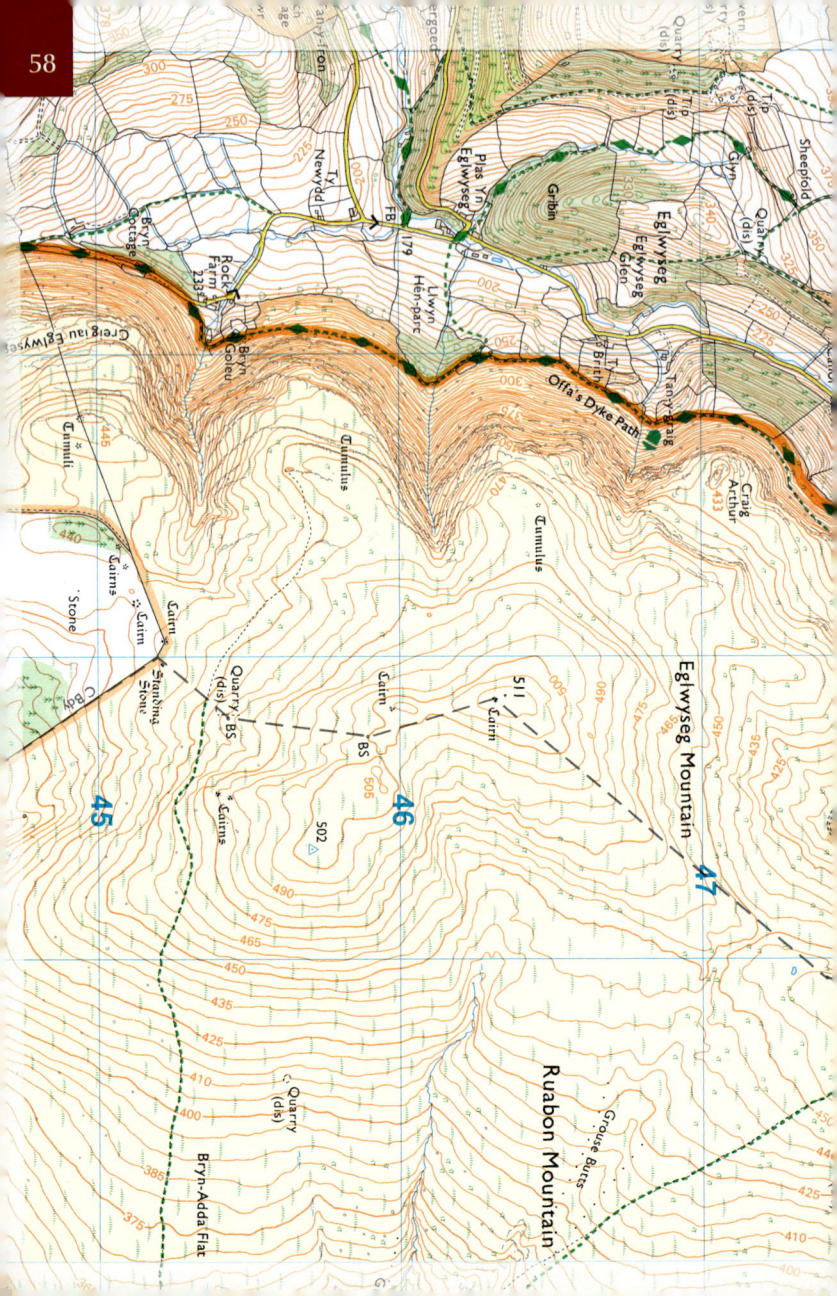

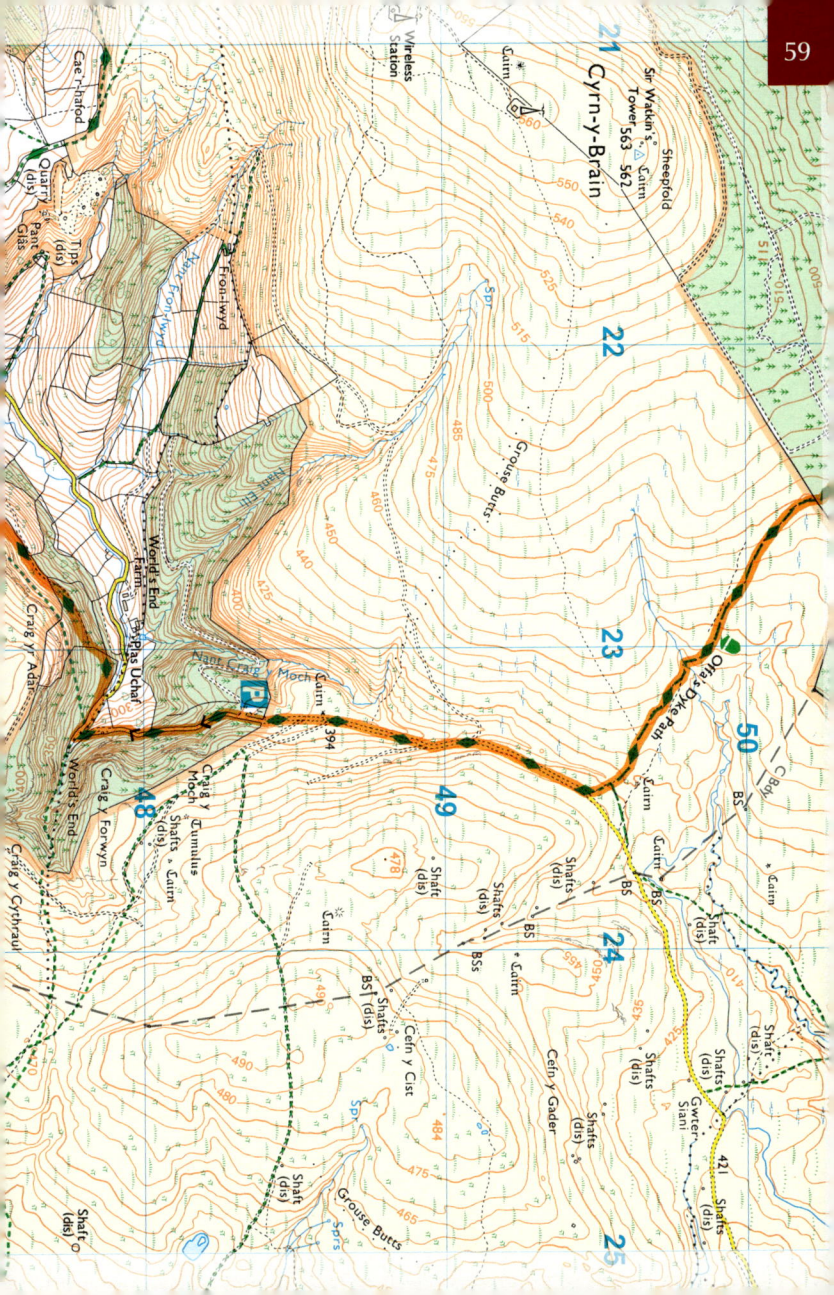

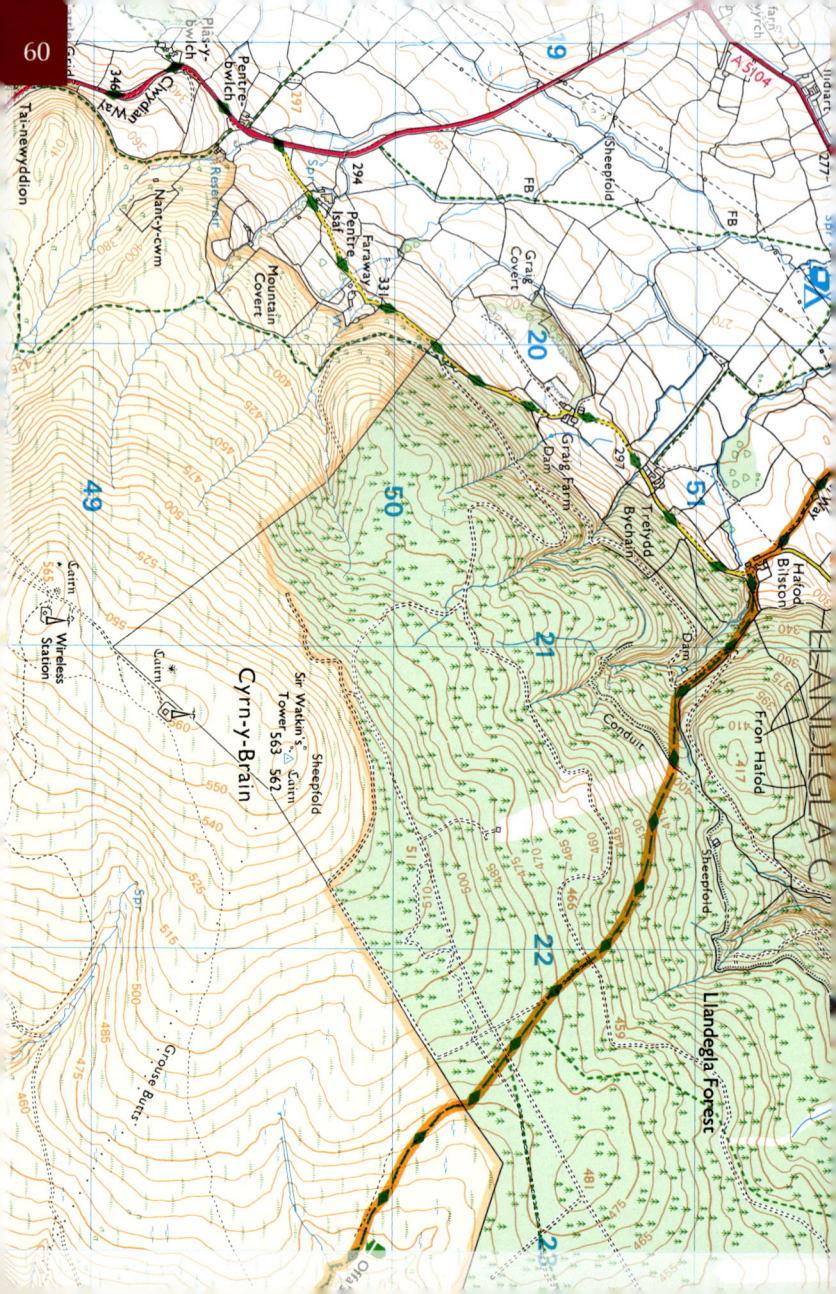

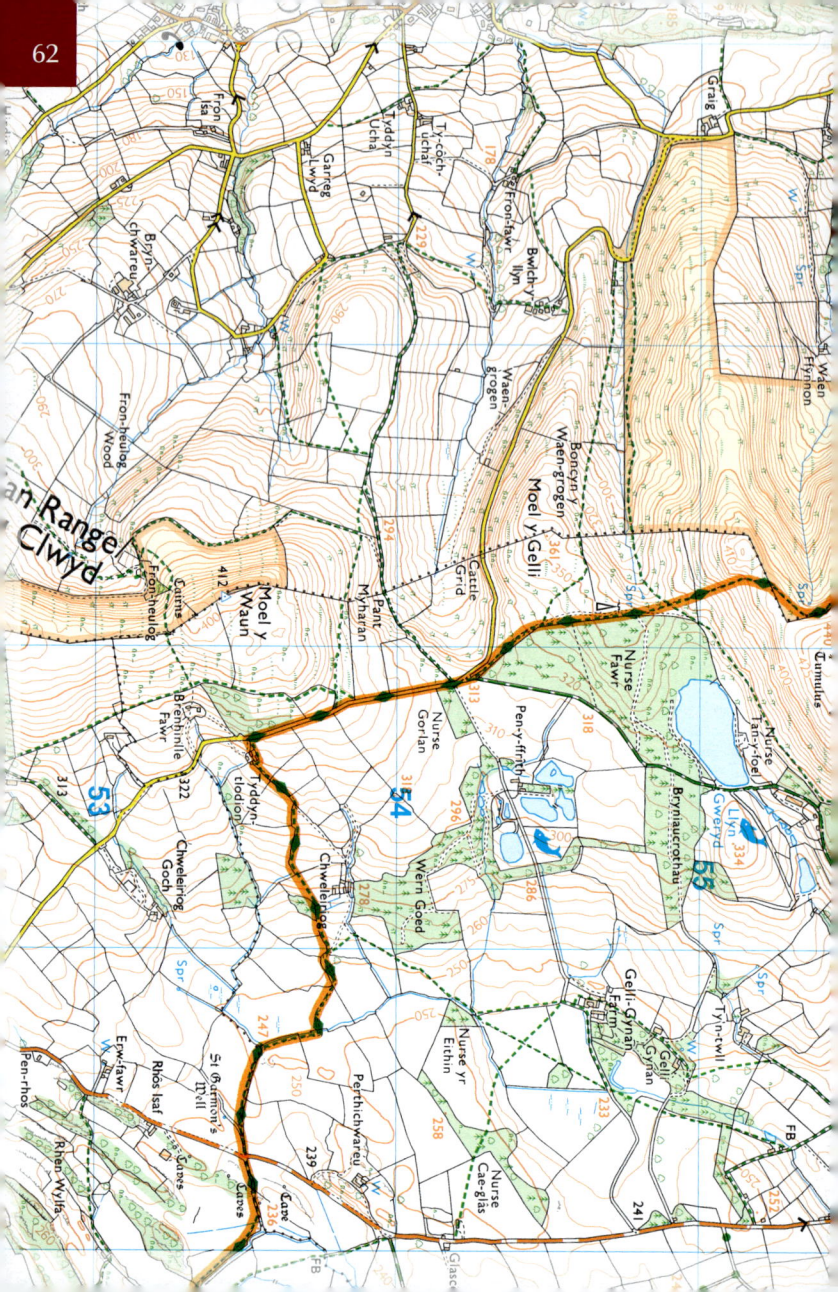

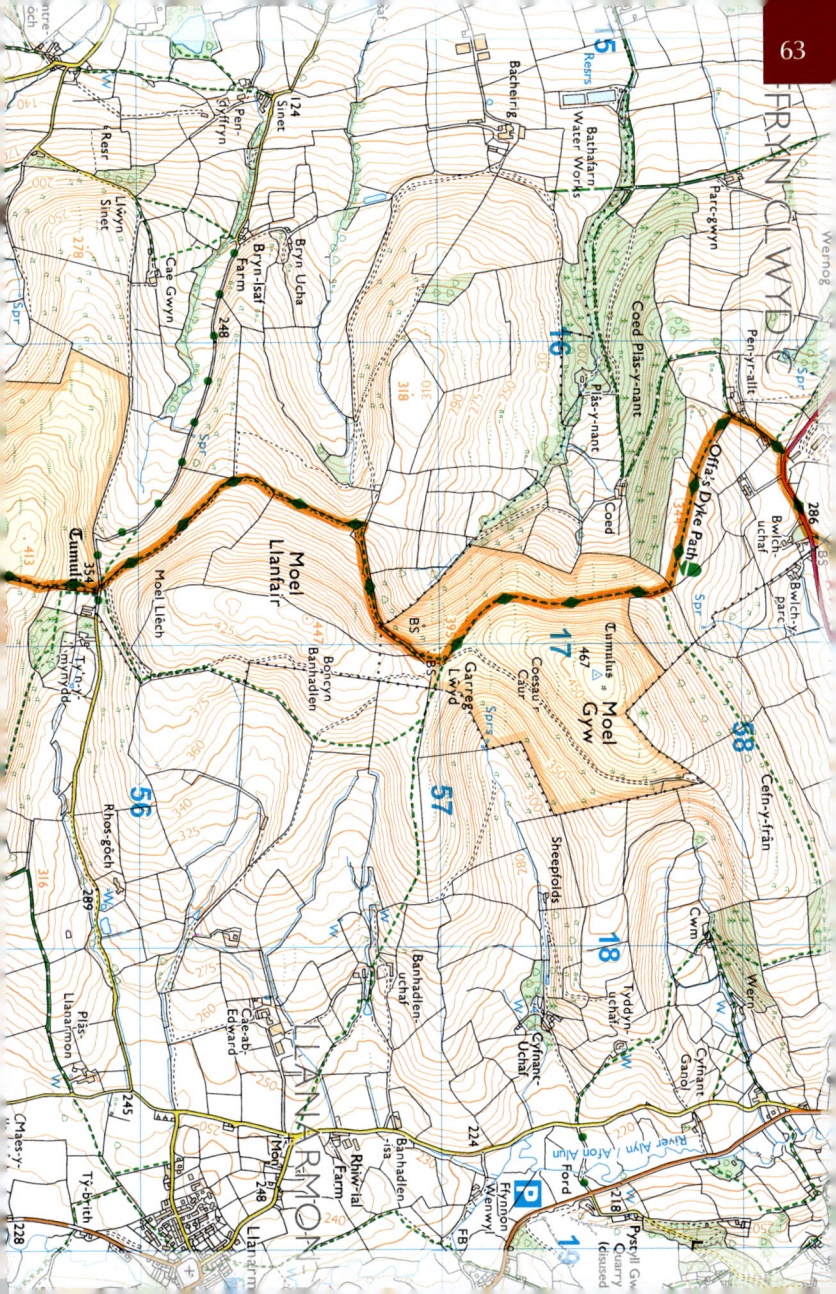

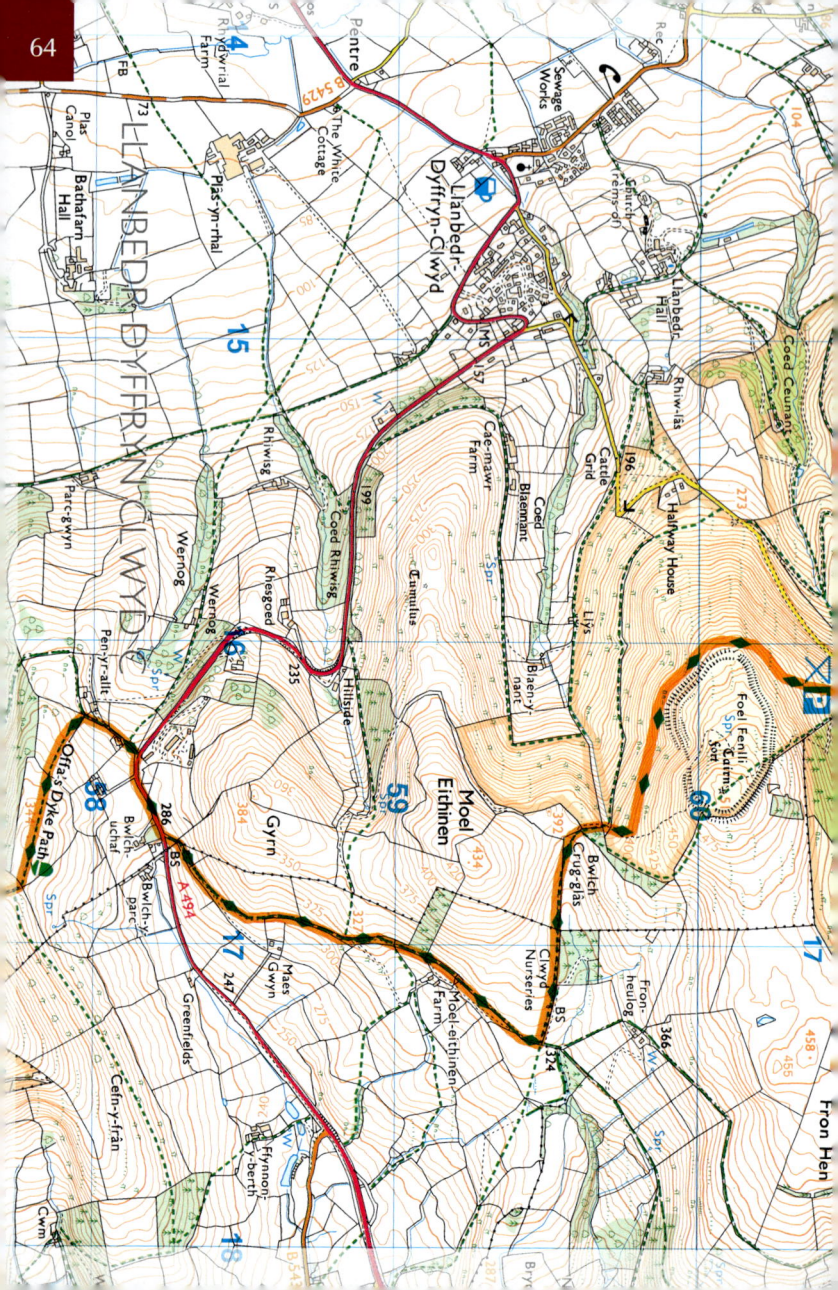

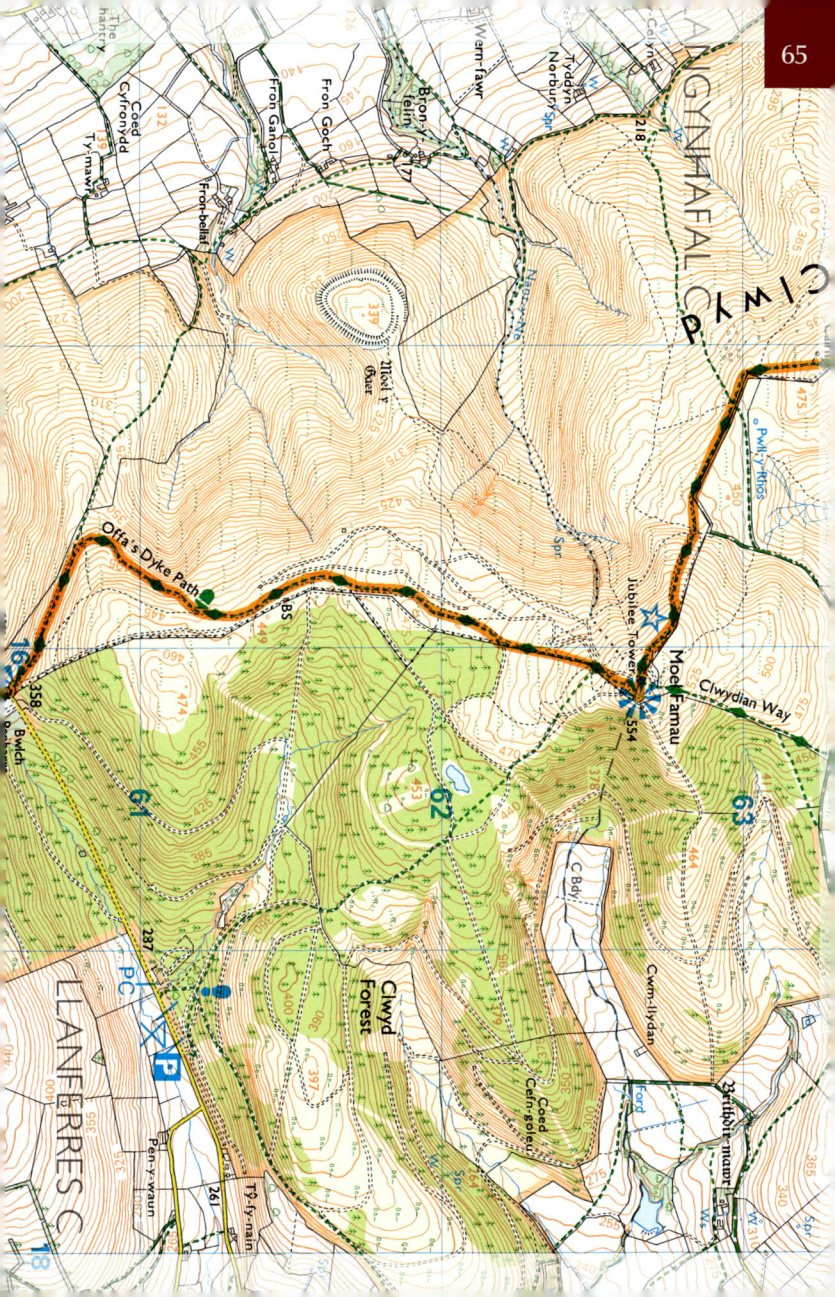

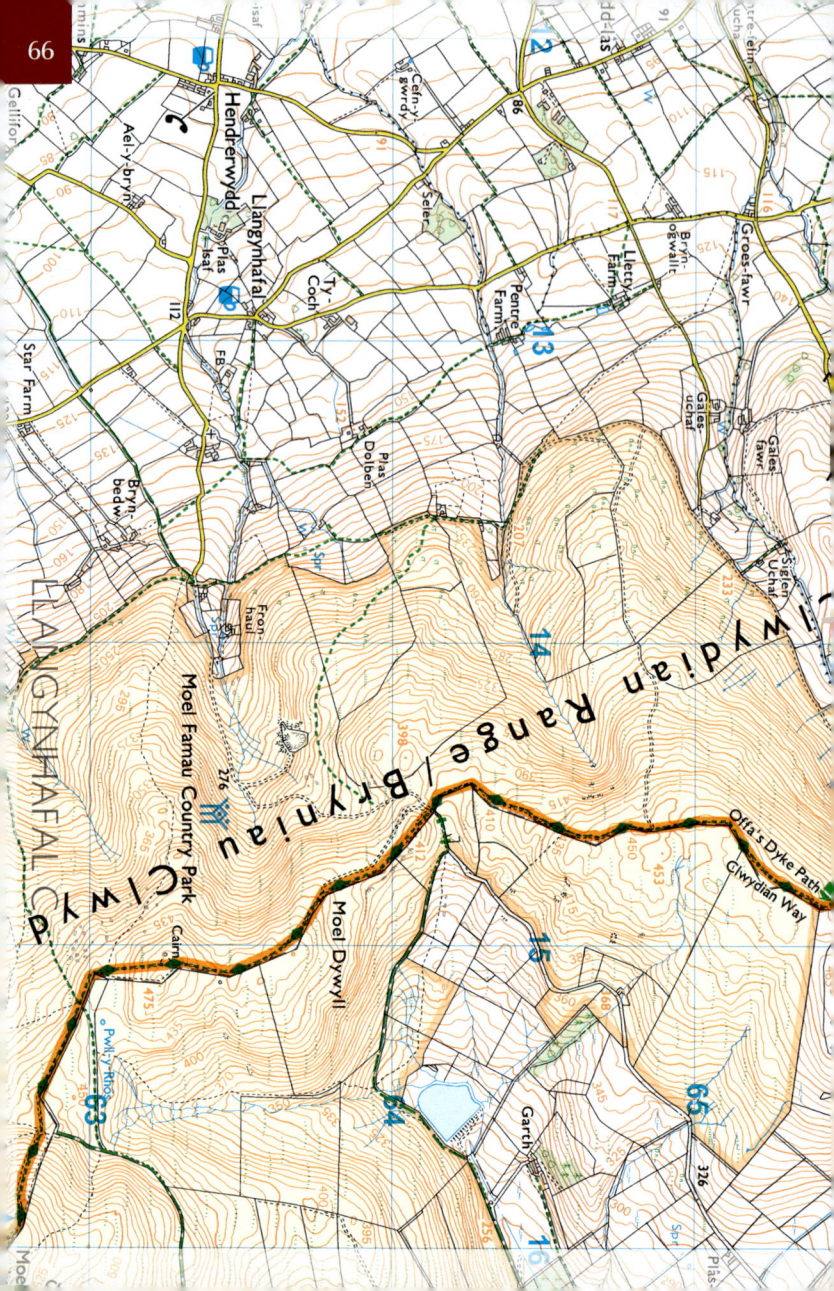

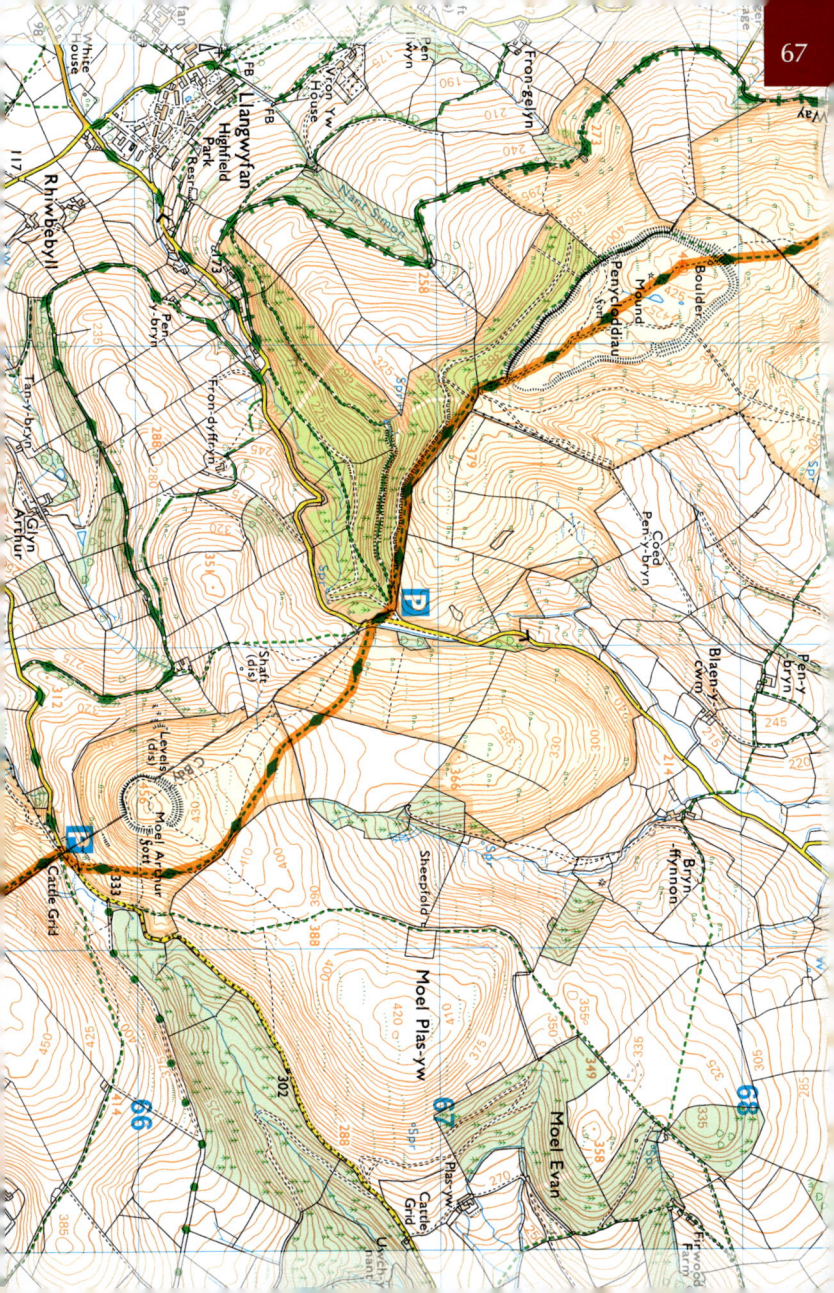

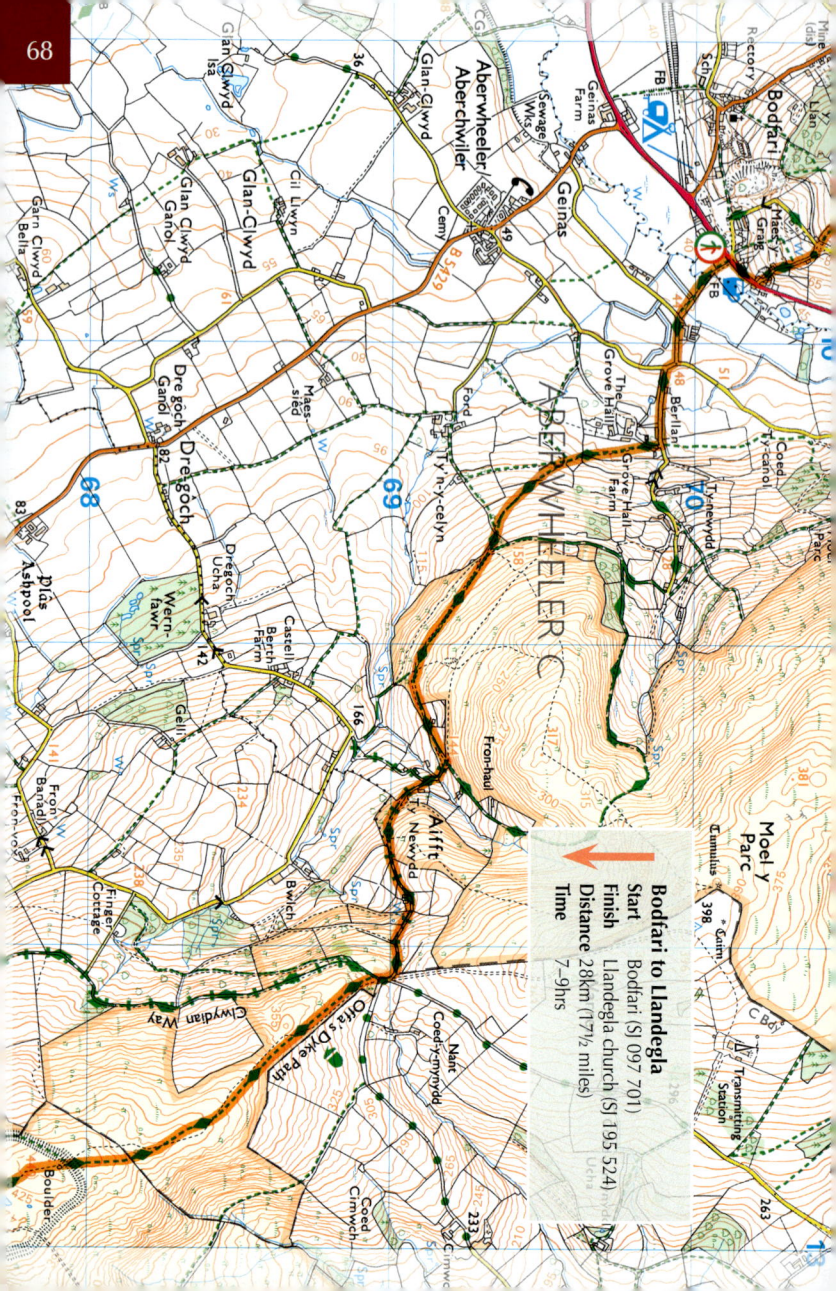

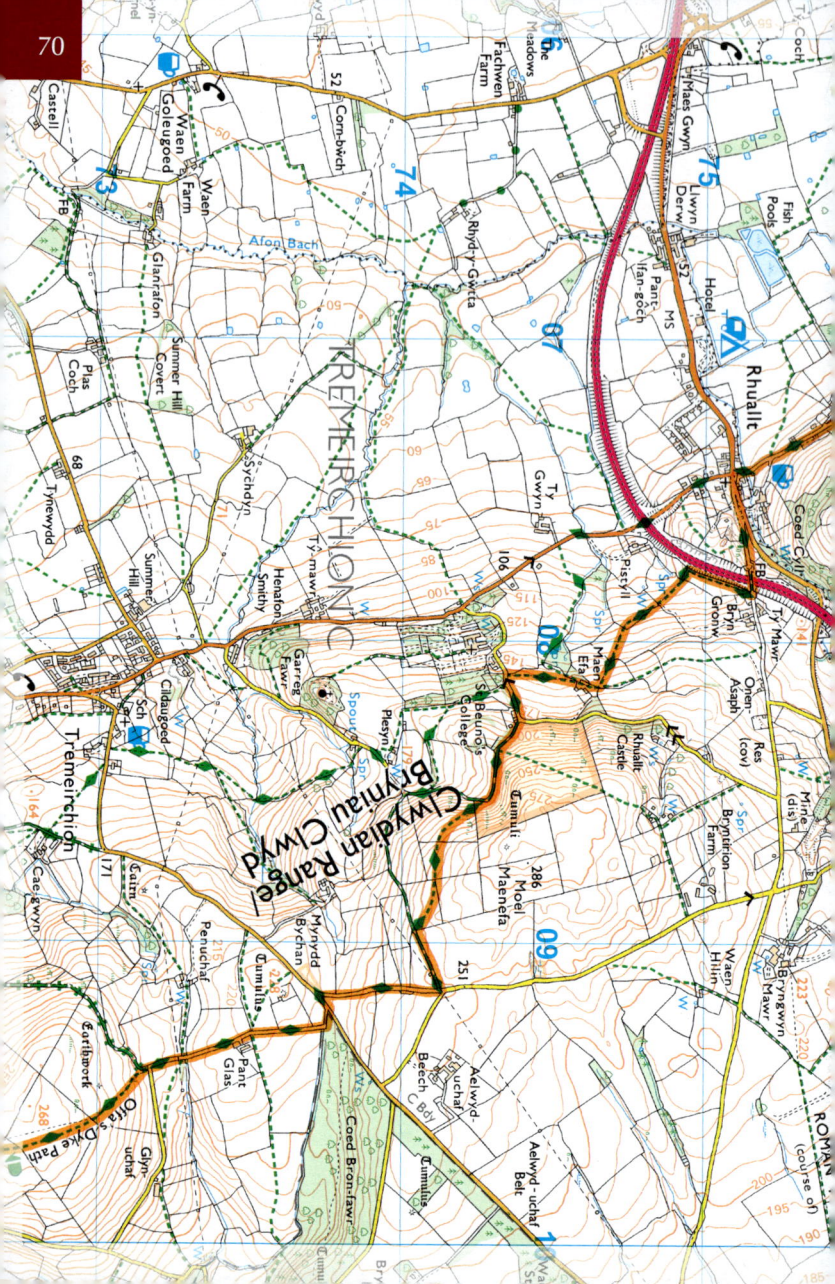

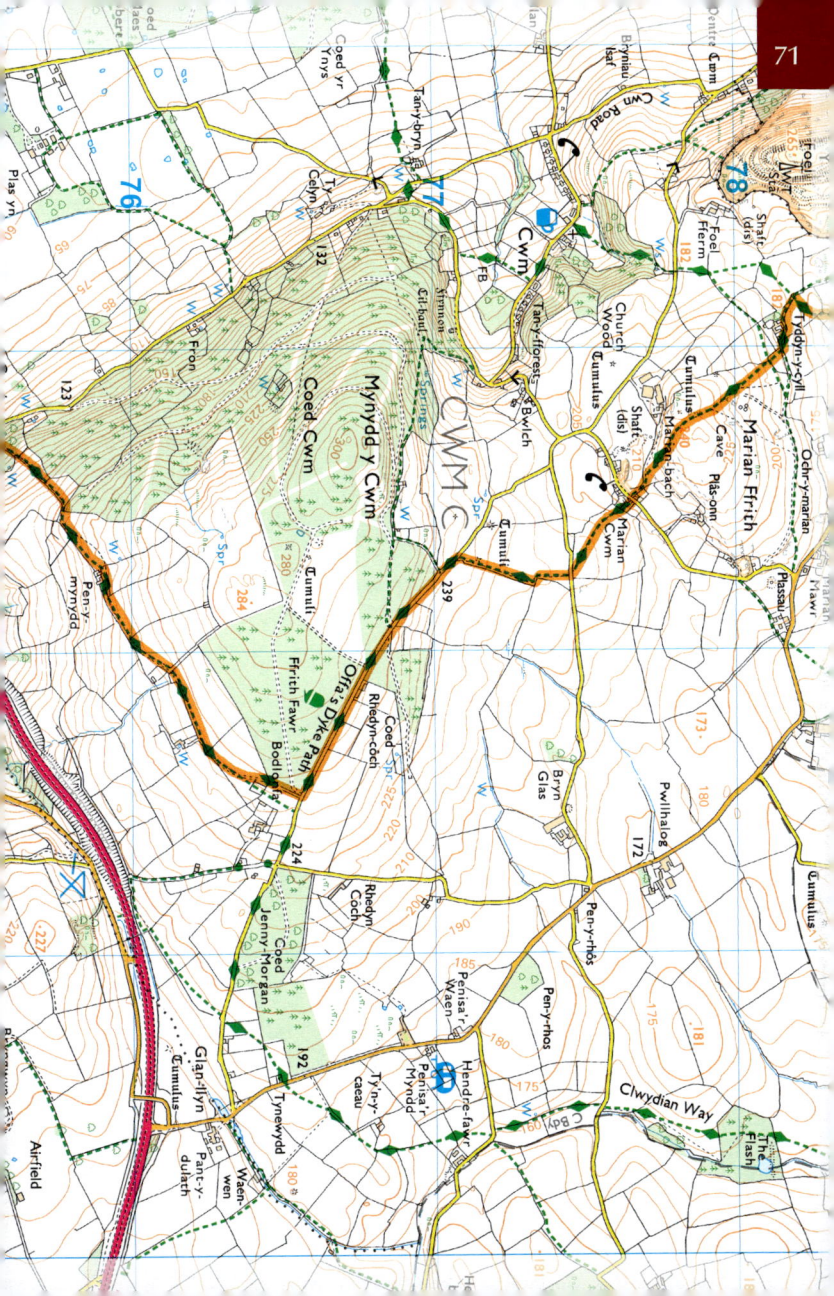

The descent from Cwm-sanaham hill to Brynorgan, with the Dyke seen climbing Llanfair hill in the background (Stage 6)

LEGEND OF SYMBOLS USED ON ORDNANCE SURVEY 1:25,000 (EXPLORER) MAPPING

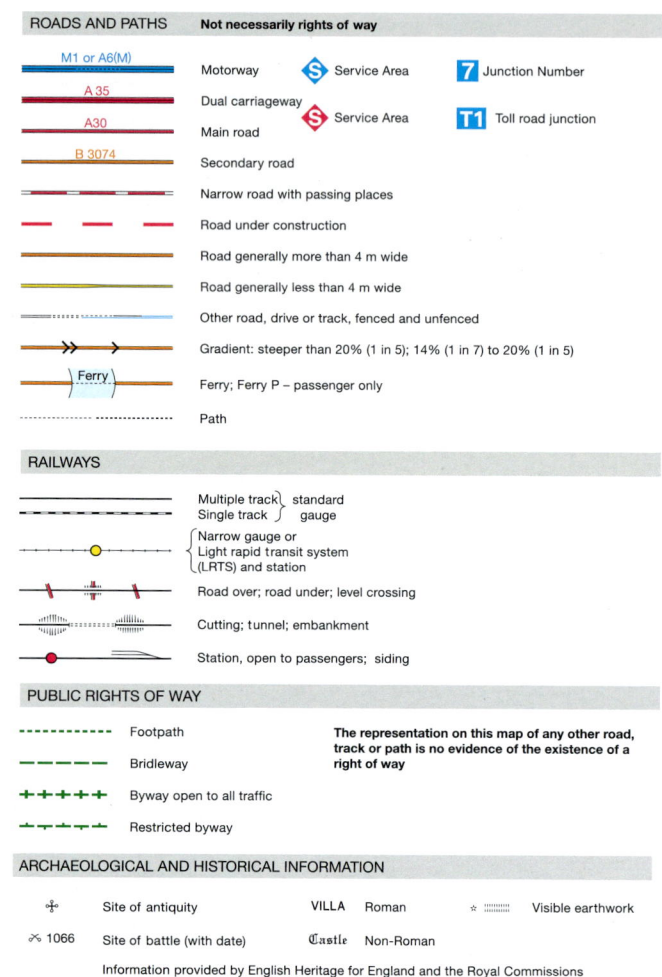

OTHER PUBLIC ACCESS

• • •	Other routes with public access	The exact nature of the rights on these routes and the existence of any restrictions may be checked with the local highway authority. Alignments are based on the best information available
♦ ♦ ♦	Recreational route	
♦ ♦ ♦	National Trail Long Distance Route	
– – – – – –	Permissive footpath	Footpaths and bridleways along which landowners have permitted public use but which are not rights of way. The agreement may be withdrawn
– – – – –	Permissive bridleway	
• • •	Traffic-free cycle route	
	National cycle network route number – traffic free; on road	

ACCESS LAND

▽DANGER AREA△	Firing and test ranges in the area. Danger! Observe warning notices		▽MANAGED ACCESS△	Access permitted within managed controls, for example, local byelaws. Visit **www.access.mod.uk** for information

England and Wales

⬠	Access land boundary and tint	Portrayal of access land on this map is intended as a guide to land which is normally available for access on foot, for example access land created under the Countryside and Rights of Way Act 2000, and land managed by the National Trust, Forestry Commission and Woodland Trust. Access for other activities may also exist. Some restrictions will apply; some land will be excluded from open access rights. The depiction of rights of access does not imply or express any warranty as to its accuracy or completeness. Observe local signs and follow the Countryside Code. Visit **www.countrysideaccess.gov.uk** for up-to-date information
▮	Access land in wooded area	
	Access information point	

BOUNDARIES

— + — + —	National
— · — · —	County (England)
— — — —	Unitary Authority (UA), Metropolitan District (Met Dist), London Borough (LB) or District (Scotland & Wales are solely Unitary Authorities)
· · · · · · · · · ·	Civil Parish (CP) (England) or Community (C) (Wales)
━ ━ ━	National Park boundary

VEGETATION

Limits of vegetation are defined by positioning of symbols

♠ ♠	Coniferous trees
♣ ♣	Non-coniferous trees
ᵒᵒ ᵒᵒ	Coppice
○ ○ ○ ○	Orchard
๐.. ๐..	Scrub
.ıllı. .ıl.	Bracken, heath or rough grassland
⌇⌇ ⌇⌇	Marsh, reeds or saltings

HEIGHTS AND NATURAL FEATURES

52 ·	Ground survey height	Surface heights are to the nearest metre above mean sea level. Where two heights are shown, the first height is to the base of the triangulation pillar and the second (in brackets) to the highest natural point of the hill
284 ·	Air survey height	

HEIGHTS AND NATURAL FEATURES (continued)

Vertical face/cliff

Loose rock | Boulders | Outcrop | Scree

Contours are at 5 or 10 metre vertical intervals

- Water
- Mud
- Sand; sand and shingle

SELECTED TOURIST AND LEISURE INFORMATION

- Building of historic interest
- Cadw
- Heritage centre
- Camp site
- Caravan site
- Camping and caravan site
- Castle / fort
- Cathedral / Abbey
- Craft centre
- Country park
- Cycle trail
- Mountain bike trail
- Cycle hire
- English Heritage
- Fishing
- Forestry Commission Visitor centre
- Garden / arboretum
- Golf course or links
- Historic Scotland
- Information centre, all year
- Information centre, seasonal
- Horse riding
- Museum
- National Park Visitor Centre (park logo) e.g. Yorkshire Dales
- Nature reserve
- National Trust
- Other tourist feature
- Parking
- Park and ride, all year
- Park and ride, seasonal
- Picnic site
- Preserved railway
- Public Convenience
- Public house/s
- Recreation / leisure / sports centre
- Roman site (Hadrian's Wall only)
- Slipway
- Telephone, emergency
- Telephone, public
- Telephone, roadside assistance
- Theme / pleasure park
- Viewpoint
- Visitor centre
- Walks / trails
- World Heritage site / area
- Water activites
- Boat trips
- Boat hire

(For complete legend and symbols, see any OS Explorer map).